THE HOLY SPIRIT COURSE:
MORE THAN JUST WORDS

A CHURCH AND SMALL GROUP
MEMBER'S MANUAL
(Second Edition)

PHILIP JANVIER

Bluebox & January

The Holy Spirit Course: More than just words
A CHURCH AND SMALL GROUP MEMBER'S MANUAL
(Second Edition)

Bluebox & January
St Stephen's Rectory
Belle Vale Road
Gateacre
Liverpool L25 2PQ
First published in the UK
by Bluebox & January
www.blueboxaudiovisual.com
blueboxandjanuary@btinternet.com

The right of Philip Janvier to be identified as the author of this work has been asserted in accordance with the Copyright, Designs and Patents Act 1988

Scripture quotations [marked NIV] taken from the Holy Bible,
New International Version Anglicised
Copyright © 1979, 1984, 2011 Biblica
Used by permission of Hodder & Stoughton Ltd,
an Hachette UK company
All rights reserved.
'NIV' is a registered trademark of Biblica UK
trademark number 1448790.

Copyright © Phil Janvier – 11th February 2017
All rights reserved.

(Second Edition)
ISBN-13: 978-1975736392
ISBN-10: 1975736397

DEDICATION

To Dorothy Williams who showed me how to minister and to God, who gives his Holy Spirit to the Church and who decided that he could use me in his service.

ALSO AVAILABLE BY PHILIP JANVIER

The Holy Spirit Course

THE HOLY SPIRIT COURSE: MORE THAN JUST WORDS – LEADER'S MANUAL (SECOND EDITION)

NINE GIFTS THAT CHANGED THE WORLD

THE HOLY SPIRIT COURSE: MORE THAN JUST WORDS – DAILY JOURNAL (FULL COLOUR)

THE HOLY SPIRIT COURSE: MORE THAN JUST WORDS – DAILY JOURNAL (PLAIN VERSION)

OUTREACH MADE EASY

Bible Study Material

HONEST BEFORE GOD – DAILY REFLECTION FROM THE HEART OF THE PSALMS

SEARCH MY HEART – DAILY REFLECTION FROM THE HEART OF THE BOOKS OF JOEL TO MALACHI

ENCOUNTERS WITH JESUS: WRITING IN THE SAND

Children's Fantasy Fiction

FIN BUTLER AND THE CLOCKWORK PHOENIX

FIN BUTLER AND THE ICE QUEEN

FIN BUTLER AND THE RELUCTANT MERMAID

Fiction

THE EMPTY PHOTOGRAPH (A NOVELLA)

Science Fiction

EMILE HAMILTON AND THE HARVEST OF SOULS

EMILE HAMILTON AND THE MUON EQUATION

'Words! Words! Words!
I'm so sick of words!
I get words all day through;
First from him,
now from you!
Sing me no song!
Read me no rhyme!
Don't waste my time,
Show me!'
(Alan Jay Lerner, Show Me, from My Fair Lady)

CONTENTS

	Acknowledgements	i
	Introduction	ii
1.	Who is the Holy Spirit?	3
2.	The Holy Spirit and You	14
3.	Introducing the Gifts of the Holy Spirit	20
4.	Gifts of Revelation	31
5.	Gifts of Power and Authority	44
6.	Gifts of Communication	57
7.	Open to God 1: The Gifts in Worship and the prayer of Boldness	68
8.	Open to God 2: The Gifts in Action	75
9.	Open to God: 3 Submission to God	83
10.	The rest of our lives	87
	Appendix: Section 1	96
	Appendix: Section 2	98
	Appendix: Section 3	100
	References	101
	Final Words	103
	About the Author	104

ACKNOWLEDGEMENTS

In preparing this material, I am entirely in the debt of two authors, Clive Calver and David Pytches. Try as I might, I have struggled to find two authors, who have captured the essence of the Holy Spirit and the gifts of the Spirit as well as they have. Clive Calver's, 'The Holy Spirit,' was first released in 1984 by the Scripture Union, a small book with a huge content. David Pytches', 'Come Holy Spirit,' published in 1985 by Hodder & Stoughton, has lived up to its subtitle, 'Learning How To Minister In Power.' I recommend both these books, and believe it is worth trawling the internet to find copies.

This book has come out of a lifetime of ministry, and I have tried, wherever possible, to quote my sources. However, a lot of my content has come from my handwritten notes, scrawled down at lectures and conferences and reproduced here. I have listed at the back of this book, all of the books I used in my initial preparation for this course, and any sources I have discovered since. If I have inadvertently failed to quote a source, I do apologise, and I request that you let me know so that I can correct that mistake in future editions.

Philip Janvier

INTRODUCTION

On Christmas Eve 1975, I found myself in my local parish church of All Soul's, Springwood. I had arrived, by mistake, half an hour early for the midnight communion. Hiding outside, I waited, until I saw a familiar face from my days as a choirboy there. Having vowed, at age 14, never to go back to church again, I found I needed to be there at Christmas. Standing next to my old friends, Clive and Jacqui, the talk and the service challenged me. So as the church bell rang in Christmas Day, I remembered praying, God I don't even know if you are there, but if you are, I want to know you!

My life changed, and I became part of an Anglican, Church of England, charismatic church. Little did I know, that the Charismatic Movement had only hit the Church of England two years before. I was dropped into the deep end of a movement of the Holy Spirit that changed the face of the church in the United Kingdom. I was influenced by amazing people like David Watson, Colin Urquhart and Michael Harper. I was there at the start of Spring Harvest, and my call to ministry came at the feet of Clive Calver, Eric Delve, Luis Palau and Graham Kendrick. I watched trends and movements sweep across the church, John Wimber and Vineyard, Toronto Blessing, Pensacola Outpouring, Signs and Wonders, they, and many that have followed, have emphasised the ministry of God, the Holy Spirit and the gifts that he brings.

I cannot imagine a church without the fruit and the gifts of the Holy Spirit being evident in it. Yet many, even within charismatic-pentecostal churches are uninformed about the third character of the Christian Trinitarian God. Some treat the Holy Spirit as an impersonal force or power, others believe that by merely speaking a set of words the Holy Spirit will act as if by magic. This Course, highly influenced by greater thinkers and theologians than me, aims to introduce people to the real person of the Holy Spirit of God.

Philip Janvier - 17th January 2017

SESSION 1
WHO IS THE HOLY SPIRIT?

When Jesus spoke to the young man in Luke's gospel, and said, *'Love the Lord your God with all your heart and with all your soul and with all your strength and with all your mind'*; and, *'Love your neighbour as yourself.' (10:27 NIV)* He was echoing those great words from Deuteronomy, *'Hear, O Israel: The Lord our God, the Lord is one. Love the Lord your God with all your heart and with all your soul and with all your strength.' (6:4-5 NIV)*

For centuries Christians have struggled to come to terms with those commandments. At the heart of the Christian is the belief in a God who is three in one, Father, the Son and the Holy Spirit. This Course was not designed to be a vehicle to teach the dynamics of the Trinity, but some understanding of it is required. As human beings, we are made in the image of God, so it should be no surprise to us, that we too are made three in one, mind, body and spirit. No matter, how good or bad, present or absent, our fathers have been, most of us have no problems in dealing with the concept of God as Father. Nor do we struggle with the idea of God as Son. However, when we come to God as the Holy Spirit, then we begin to have problems. This Course is aimed at helping us discover a little more about the third member of the Trinity and his role in the church.

The Holy Spirit
When Jesus left his disciples here on earth, he promised them that he would send the Comforter, the Holy Spirit, who would be like Jesus and would live in them.

DISCUSSION:
In fiction, characters are often described as being unreal. What are the principle characteristics that define someone as a real person?

1. A Real Person
- He is a person - distinct from the Father and the Son.
- Not an alien force or influence or magic.
- He is God - sharing the divine nature with the Father and the Son.

This is important because:
- He can be known experientially.
- He is not an unknown power to be got hold of and used, but a person who desires to be part of our lives.
- In the context of the Godhead, he is to be worshipped.

2. His Personality

Although the Holy Spirit is a person, it does not mean he has to have a body, but he does have a personality.

- **Person - Teacher and Guide**

John 14:26, *But the Advocate, the Holy Spirit, whom the Father will send in my name, will teach you all things and will remind you of everything I have said to you. (NIV).*

John 15:26 *'When the Advocate comes, whom I will send to you from the Father – the Spirit of truth who goes out from the Father – he will testify about me. (NIV)*

John 16:13&14 *But when he, the Spirit of truth, comes, he will guide you into all the truth. He will not speak on his own; he will speak only what he hears, and he will tell you what is yet to come. He will glorify me because it is from me that he will receive what he will make known to you. (NIV)*

- **Emotion**

Grief - Ephesians 4:30 *And do not grieve the Holy Spirit of God, with whom you were sealed for the day of redemption. (NIV)*

Love - Romans 15:30 *I urge you, brothers and sisters, by our Lord Jesus Christ and by the love of the Spirit, to join me in my struggle by praying to God for me. (NIV)*

- **Knowledge and Intelligence**

Romans 8:*27 And he who searches our hearts knows the mind of the Spirit because the Spirit intercedes for God's people in accordance with the will of God.(NIV)*

Acts 15:28 *It seemed good to the Holy Spirit and to us not to burden you with anything beyond the following requirements (NIV)*

John 14:26, *But the Advocate, the Holy Spirit, whom the Father will send in my name, will teach you all things and will remind you of everything I have said to you. (NIV)*

Revelation 2:7 *Whoever has ears, let them hear what the Spirit says to the churches. To the one who is victorious, I will give the right to eat from the tree of life, which is in the paradise of God. (NIV)*

Romans 8:*26 In the same way, the Spirit helps us in our weakness. We do not know what we ought to pray for, but the Spirit himself intercedes for us through wordless groans. (NIV)*

- **Will**

Acts 13:2 *While they were worshipping the Lord and fasting, the Holy Spirit said, 'Set apart for me Barnabas and Saul for the work to which I have called them.' (NIV)*

1 Corinthians 12:11 *All these are the work of one and the same Spirit, and he distributes them to each one, just as he determines. (NIV)*

John 3:8 *The wind blows wherever it pleases. You hear its sound, but you cannot tell where it comes from or where it is going. So it is with everyone born of the Spirit.' (NIV)*

3. His Divinity

- In creation

Genesis 1:2 *Now the earth was formless and empty, darkness was over the surface of the deep, and the Spirit of God was hovering over the waters. (NIV)*

Psalms 33:6 *By the word of the LORD the heavens were made,*
   their starry host by the breath of his mouth. (NIV)

Job 26:13 *By his breath the skies became fair;*
   his hand pierced the gliding serpent. (NIV)

Genesis 2:7 *Then the LORD God formed a man from the dust of the ground and breathed into his nostrils the breath of life, and the man became a living being. (NIV)*

- **Knowledge**

1 Corinthians 2:10 *these are the things God has revealed to us by his Spirit. The Spirit searches all things, even the deep things of God. (NIV)*

- **Presence**

Psalm 139:7-10 *Where can I go from your Spirit?*
   Where can I flee from your presence?
If I go up to the heavens, you are there;
   if I make my bed in the depths, you are there.
If I rise on the wings of the dawn,
   if I settle on the far side of the sea,
even there your hand will guide me,
   your right hand will hold me fast (NIV)

- **Eternal**

Hebrews 9:14 *How much more, then, will the blood of Christ, who through the eternal Spirit offered himself unblemished to God, cleanse our consciences from acts that lead to death, so that we may serve the living God! (NIV)*

The same Holy Spirit who worked through the Lord Jesus Christ is the same Holy Spirit who dwells, inhabits and lives in the Church - the Body of Christ, to enable it to reflect and to live in the character of Jesus and to fulfil the ministry of the Lord Jesus in the world.

When we come to Christ, the person of the Holy Spirit comes to live in us to link us into the body of Christ, and to enable us to fill our part in it fully and comprehensively. He is the giver of gifts, the bringer of love and it is the Spirit who enables us to cry out 'Abba Father.'

GOD THE HOLY SPIRIT IN THE OLD TESTAMENT.

DISCUSSION:
Can you suggest any examples of God the Holy Spirit that are evident in the Old Testament?

In the Old Testament, God the Holy Spirit's personality is hardly considered. In many ways, he is seen as an impersonal force such as when he is described as ruach, the wind or force of God.

However, his personality is expressed in other ways by his activities:

- **The Spirit broods**, Genesis 1:*2*

- **He acts in creation** by creating human beings. Genesis 2:7

As we move through the Old Testament higher qualities of personalities or humanity are shown.

- **Administration qualities** are given to Joseph Genesis 39:6

- **Military genius** is given to Gideon Judges 7:7.

- **Craftsmanship** Exodus 34:28

His influence goes on in inspiration, intelligence, righteousness, ethical profits and in holiness.

The Holy Spirit, he is more than just an influence, and there are hints of more:
- Haggai 2:5,

- Zechariah 4:6,

- Isaiah 48:16.
  Endowed by the Spirit

- Isaiah 63:10&11

Ultimately, his personality is shown in his holiness of which there are many and various references, but particularly in Psalm 51: 11 *Do not cast me from your presence or take your Holy Spirit from me. (NIV)* and Isaiah 63: 10. *Yet they rebelled and grieved his Holy Spirit. So he turned and became their enemy and he himself fought against them. (NIV)*

The Old Testament does not allow or encourage us to read the Trinity back into its pages, although God the Holy Spirit is there. The Spirit, as distinct from God the Father and God the Son is a New Testament doctrine but based on Old Testament understanding. What is clear, is that the Spirit in the Old Testament comes upon the chosen people of God but does not fill them permanently in the way we have grown to understand. This distinction of filling is an indication of the end times, a time we are now living in.

GOD THE HOLY SPIRIT IN THE NEW TESTAMENT.

DISCUSSION: If God the Holy Spirit is evident in the New Testament, what examples can you remember?

1. The Early Ministry of Jesus.
There are three special occasions when God the Holy Spirit is emphasised:
- At the Baptism of Jesus

When the Spirit falls upon the person of Jesus himself. To consecrate him as Messiah, and to symbolise the beginning of the new covenant.

Luke 3:20-22

- **At the temptation**
Matthew 4:1

• **At the preaching at Nazareth**
Luke 4:18

Isaiah 61:1

2. **Jesus refers to the Holy Spirit**
Matthew 12:28

Mark 3:29

Luke 11:13

John 14:26

Luke 10: 21

Luke 24: 49

Matthew 28: 19

3. **The Holy Spirit in John's Teaching.**
The Apostle John is quite keen to show the Holy Spirit as being someone who is personally and closely associated with the redeeming work of Christ.

John 1:32-34

John 3:5-8
_____
_____
_____

- In the discourse with the Samaritan woman at the well, Jesus describes the Holy Spirit as living water.

John 4:14
_____
_____
_____

John describes the Holy Spirit as the Paraclete (Advocate, comforter, etc.) who takes over the role of the Son of Man and carries out his work. The Holy Spirit becomes the presence of God.
John 14: 16
_____
_____
_____

4. The Acts of the Holy Spirit.

In the Book of Acts, there are at least seventeen references to the Holy Spirit, and as a result, the Acts of the Apostles could be renamed the Acts of the Holy Spirit.

- Three features of the Book of Acts stand out.

A) The Disciples teaching is concentrated on the Lordship of Christ and on the Holy Spirit.

Acts 1:2
_____
_____
_____

Acts 1:4
_____
_____
_____

Acts 1:8
_____
_____
_____

B). The second feature is the promise given to the Day of Pentecost Acts 2: 22-36. It was the vindication of Christ to the Jewish people and the demonstration of his character and claim.

Acts 2:33
_____
_____
_____

- **It brought a new power to the Disciples.**
Acts 4: 33
_____
_____
_____
_____

9

- It was the entrance of the Holy Spirit into human lives to make real the work of Christ.

C) It gave a prominence to the Spirit of God in the early Church.

The Work of the Spirit in the Believer

- **Pre-conversion**
Acts 2:38

- **Re-generation**
John 3:5

Titus 3:5

Romans 8:15

- **Spirit of Sonship**
Galatians 4:6

- **Indwelling**
1 Corinthians 3:16

1 Corinthians 6:19

Romans 8:9

- **Makes Christians, changes people into the likeness of Christ.**
John 16:14

- **Spirit of freedom**

- **Spirit of Prayer,**
Romans 8:26

- **Spirit of Correction**
Ephesians 4:30

_____
_____
_____
_____

1 Thessalonians 5:23

_____
_____
_____
_____

- **Spirit of Growth**
Galatians 5:22

_____
_____

The Holy Spirit Expresses:
- **Adoption**
Romans 8:14

_____
_____
_____

- **Seals**
Ephesians 1:13

_____
_____
_____

- **Sanctifies**
1 Peter 1: 2

_____
_____

Corinthians 14:12

_____
_____
_____
_____
_____

- **Gifts of the Spirit**
1 Corinthians 12:7

_____
_____
_____
_____
_____
_____

- **The Fruit**
Galatians 5:22

_____
_____
_____

- **Service**
1 Corinthians 12:7

_____
_____
_____
_____

DISCUSSION QUESTIONS:

1. What would it have been like to have heard Jesus say? *But the Advocate, the Holy Spirit, whom the Father will send in my name, will teach you all things and will remind you of everything I have said to you. (John 14:26 NIV).*
2. What do you think the Apostle Paul meant when he wrote? *And do not grieve the Holy Spirit of God, with whom you were sealed for the day of redemption. (Ephesians 4:30 NIV)*
3. Describe a time when you have felt anxious and have wanted God to be near you. *Do not cast me from your presence or take your Holy Spirit from me. (Psalm 51: 11 NIV)*
4. What do you think Jesus meant when he said? *I am going to send you what my Father has promised; but stay in the city until you have been clothed with power from on high. (Luke 24: 49 NIV)*
5. How did Jesus describe the Holy Spirit?

Conclusion

In conclusion, when we come to Christ, the Holy Spirit comes to live in us to knit us into the body and to enable us to fulfil our part in it.

All of this begs two questions; 'Can you have a church without the Holy Spirit?' and 'Can you be a Christian without the Holy Spirit?'

Without the Holy Spirit of God, there would be no worship, because only those who worship God in spirit and truth can worship God. Therefore all we would be left with would be ritual and habit. No understanding, because the Spirit is the bringer of all truth. No witness, because we would be left to our own resources. No power, either in our own lives, or that of the Church. No gifts, because only God the Holy Spirit equips us for service. We could go on, there would be no life, no future, no uniqueness, no guidance, no security, no evidence and finally and ultimately no Resurrection! Christianity without the Holy Spirit just would not exist.

It is impossible for us to understand all that God has to give us in worship, witness, service and the spiritual gifts unless we know something of the person of the Holy Spirit.

Reflection on Session 1

- What has God shown me?

- What do I need to ask God for?

- What do I need to do?

- Other comments.

Notes:

SESSION 2
THE HOLY SPIRIT AND YOU

May the grace of the Lord Jesus Christ, and the love of God, and the fellowship of the Holy Spirit be with you all. (2 Corinthians 13:14 NIV)

These familiar words speak of the fellowship that we have with the Holy Spirit. That fellowship is the sharing of our lives with God and each other. God enables us to do this through the work of the Holy Spirit, he goes between Jesus and us. As a direct consequence of his action, he shares Jesus life, love and power with us. The Spirit enables us to love the Lord our God with all our heart, soul, mind and strength, and our neighbours as ourselves. The Holy Spirit is the bringer of fellowship, maintainer of relationships, and the channel both with Jesus and with each other. The Holy Spirit is the sustainer and equipper of the Church. This work began in the Church on the Day of Pentecost and has continued until today.

For many people, Jesus Christ is merely a good example of how to live. However, if we were live our Christian lives with Jesus merely an example, this would reduce us quickly to despair. Jesus made a promise - God the Holy Spirit would be with us empowering and equipping and revealing Jesus to each new generation of disciples. That promise was kept on the Day of Pentecost when the Spirit came down on all believers. That promise still applies today.

How do I know the Holy Spirit is in my life?

The first sign that God, the Holy Spirit is in someone's life is not a complete and final change in that person's character. Nor is it that person receiving a new set of spiritual gifts. Instead, it is two heartfelt, radically honest confessions of faith.

a)   The Christian will confess that Jesus is Lord.
 Paul in the Scriptures tells us that we can only say this with the help of the Holy Spirit.
Romans 10:9
_____
_____

b)   The Christian be able to call God 'Abba Father.'
The Spirit teaches us that we are God's children and that we have the right, along with Jesus, to call him daddy.
Romans 8:15
_____
_____

Amazingly enough, the two simple confessions are all the proof that we need in a new disciples life or an old disciples life, that the Holy Spirit is present and active.

Actions of the Spirit.

Whenever we move into the area of the Spiritual Gifts, we find ourselves moving from the realm of the natural to the supernatural. For many people when they first hear about such gifts, find this whole concept to be a bit strange and spiritualistic.

Yet there are essential differences between the counterfeits of the devil and the incredible supernatural gifts that God alone gives through the Holy Spirit. God, the Holy Spirit, does not take away the power of control or, as in spiritualism, does the individual need to have an empty mind. The Christian when using the Spiritual Gifts is hoping and seeking to fill their mind and heart with the Glory of Jesus Christ. This is not so that we become less, but so that we become more. At no point can a Christian plead 'I couldn't help it,' because the Holy Spirit actually develops our self-control. *For the Spirit God gave us does not make us timid, but gives us power, love and self-discipline. (2 Timothy1:7 NIV)*

If a particular gift takes a person over you can be certain this is from the evil one, and it is not a gift from God and should be rejected as such. Also, all Spiritual Gifts are subject to be tested, they do not carry any absolute authority.

The spirits of prophets are subject to the control of prophets. (1 Corinthians 14:32 NIV)

We need never fear the supernatural when God is concerned because what happens is that the Spirit of God encourages the person involved to express the supernatural in the most natural of ways. The Gifts of the Spirit always build up the Church. We need not ever be afraid, and in fact, in the Scriptures, we are told that. *There is no fear in love. But perfect love drives out fear, because fear has to do with punishment. The one who fears is not made perfect in love. (1 John 4:18 NIV)*

'Being filled with the Holy Spirit.'

'Baptism in the Holy Spirit is that aspect of Christian initiation in which through expectant and appropriating faith in Christ's promise, the indwelling Holy Spirit manifest himself in our experience, so that he works in and through us with freedom and effectiveness in the manhood of Christ.' (Tom Smail, Reflected Glory)

This experience is often accompanied by a gift of the Holy Spirit, for example, the gift of tongue, which enables us to speak directly with God, increased fellowship and a new desire to witness effectively.

Four Possible Dangers:

1. The division of God's believing people into first and second class citizens.
Galatians 3:28

2. Making a false distinction between conversion and baptism in the Spirit.

3. Applying false conditions onto a free gift of God, this contractual approach is deeply entrenched in much charismatic renewal. *'It holds that the Spirit and his gifts are given when we have repented enough, prayed enough, claimed enough, "tarried" enough.'* *(Tom Smail; Reflected Glory)*

4. Making a law out of one experience, when the New Testament is filled with a great variety of experience. For example, the Gift of the Spirit is described as:

- **As a promise and a gift,**
Acts 1:4

- **A baptism,**
Acts 1:5

- **Something you will receive,**
Acts 1:8

- **Something that is poured out,**
Acts 2:17

Notes:

Three Basic Truths.

1. To describe the Holy Spirit as Gift emphasises that we are here in the realm of grace. We are reminded that we are not in the normal world that calculates its benefits in proportion to conditions fulfilled, but in the Kingdom of a gracious loving father who generously gives his Holy Spirit in free unconditional grace, and undeserved free gift, who recognises we cannot and have not earned such a gift and yet out of his generosity opens the way and prepares for us to receive the Holy Spirit.

2. To describe the Holy Spirit as a 'Gift of Grace' emphasises that we are in a dynamic relationship with God himself. We are in a relationship in which we receive an exceptionally generous giver. The fact that we are aware that the Holy Spirit to us is a gift reminds us that he cannot be studied in isolation from God himself. As a gift is meaningless without a giver and receiver. It is only in a direct relationship with the giver of the gifts can we know the Holy Spirit.

3. When we describe the Holy Spirit as a 'Gift of Grace' we recognise that we in the individual's personal realm. God gives the Holy Spirit in the context of a personal relationship and as an expression of his love for his people. It is also, in this case, the gift is himself a person and as such giver is giving nothing less than himself. *'The value of this gift is that the one who is given wills to be given, and he comes to us as one who has the divine willingness to give. He is the giving of gift.' (Tom Smail, Reflected Glory)*

Notes:

What the Holy Spirit's Renewal and Refreshment brings to the Church.
1. The rediscovery of the supernatural gifts that God gives his church.
2. A fresh appreciation of the Bible as the Word of God.
3. Relaxed but reverent, collaborative praise, prayer and worship.
4. The use of Spiritual Gifts by every Christian.
5. A desire to bring the whole person, body, mind and spirit, through acts of public, and private, prayer and worship into the presence of God, the Holy Spirit.
6. A rediscovery of evangelism and outreach, matched with acts of service.
7. The exploration of ministry through a caring and more communal life.
8. That God is longing to give gifts and that the church will see miracles, and receive messages, visions, supernatural healings and similar manifestations

With a fresh emphasis on:
9. A new sense of belonging.
10. Radical Honesty, a new sense of sharing our joys, pains, successes and failures.
11. Every Member Ministry - We all have gifts that build each other up
12. Fellowship, small groups that can be nurseries for spiritual gifts, a place to develop and grow together, in an environment of loving trust. As well as a place to grow together through Bible study and prayer.

DISCUSSION QUESTIONS:

What do you think the Apostle Paul meant when he wrote? *May the grace of the Lord Jesus Christ, and the love of God, and the fellowship of the Holy Spirit be with you all. (2 Corinthians 13:14 NIV)*

1. Can you describe a time when you noticed the Holy Spirit working in your church or community?
2. How do you react when you hear the word 'supernatural' used in church?
3. What do you think the prophet meant when he said? *"In the last days, God says, I will pour out my Spirit on all people. Your sons and daughters will prophesy, your young men will see visions, your old men will dream dreams. (Acts 2:17 NIV.)*
4. Describe a time when you felt physically or emotionally a second class Christian.

Reflection on Session 2

- **What has God shown me?**

- **What do I need to ask God for?**

- **What do I need to do?**

- **Other comments.**

Notes:

SESSION 3
INTRODUCING THE GIFTS OF THE HOLY SPIRIT

Introduction:
A story - A Christian raised his head around and realised that finally, he had crossed the vast gulf between life on earth and life in heaven. He walks off to the gates of heaven and is warmly greeted by the Archangel Gabriel who having shaken hands, (after all he was English,) offered the Christian a personal guided tour around the sites of heaven. They began their journey through a section of enormous hangers, giant warehouses, stacked with shelf after shelf after shelf. Each shelf was filled with row upon row of beautifully wrapped presents. Each one of them had the Christians name. The Christian stood still for a moment and looked around amazed, overawed by the generosity of God. 'What's all this?' he asked the Archangel Gabriel. 'These,' replied the Archangel, 'are all the gifts which God had chosen to give you on earth which you never bothered to claim or use!'

God, the Holy Spirit, is the greatest gift that God can give. God gives Himself. If we reject or ignore the gifts which God gives, we are insulting Him, damaging both the relationship we have with God and with others. For the spiritual gifts are not designed to be used for the benefit of ourselves, but are instead meant, as tools for the Kingdom, for the benefit of others and of the Church. It is only when we use the gifts which God gives, that we clearly show the reality of the living Church of the Lord Jesus Christ. We are the body of Christ here on earth, gifted even as Christ was gifted. But even Jesus said, *Very truly I tell you, whoever believes in me will do the works I have been doing, and they will do even greater things than these, because I am going to the Father. (John 14.12 NIV)* So we miss out on these gifts at our peril.

Exercise: Share with the group examples of your natural gifts. If you know the members of your group, tell them what you think their main gifts are.

Natural Gifts

Every human being is a unique individual created in the image of God. Each person is different and possesses different natural gifts, talents and abilities. Although some are more obvious than others, there is nobody who is without natural gifts of one particular sort or another. These gifts, whether physical, academic or other can either be used to further our own ends or be given to God. The Holy Spirit is able to use the natural gifts of those who have discovered the Lordship of Christ in their lives. The Holy Spirit takes what is already there and strengthens, broadens, and uses it for his work in the Church and the world. On occasions, God will manifest Himself through a person in a way independent of their natural ability. That is why, in looking at the Spiritual Gifts, it's hard sometimes to categorise natural from the supernatural.

Supernatural Gifts

However, it is apparent that the gifts listed in 1 Corinthians 12 where clearly of a supernatural form and as a result were the most controversial. The gifts are mentioned in a variety of places:

1 Corinthians 12
This passage is too long to place here, but Pauls begins with these words:
Now about the gifts of the Spirit, brothers and sisters, I do not want you to be uninformed. (1 Corinthians 12.1 NIV)
Romans 12: 6-8
We have different gifts, according to the grace given to each of us. If your gift is prophesying, then prophesy in accordance with your faith; [7] if it is serving, then serve; if it is teaching, then teach; [8] if it is to encourage, then give encouragement; if it is giving, then give generously; if it is to lead, do it diligently; if it is to show mercy, do it cheerfully. (NIV)
Ephesians 4
But to each one of us grace has been given as Christ apportioned it. (7 NIV)
1 Peter 4: 10.
Each of you should use whatever gift you have received to serve others, as faithful stewards of God's grace in its various forms. (NIV)
As we look at all these particular references, we need to be careful of labels

and categories. Nobody fits into just one category, and we must recognise that God Himself is the source and we are the channels of his Grace.

We, as the body of Christ, will only function properly when each of us fulfils our part, however, great or small or apparently insignificant. One person's gifts are not more valuable than others.

EXERCISE: 1

Test your gifts

In the first horizontal row of three squares consider the four lines that describe you best and place a number 3 in that square. Then repeat the process scoring 2 for the next appropriate and 1 for the least. Repeat this exercise for each horizontal row.

Thoughtful Intelligent Rational Open to Reason	Spontaneous Adventurous Risk-taker Explorer	Co-operative Motivator Visionary Authentic
Intuitive Confident in God Can make difficult choices I can apply spiritual truth	Explorer My prayers are answered God does the incredible in me I expect signs & wonders	Inspirational I pray in tongues God gives me messages I expect to hear God
I know when God is working I can sense the Holy Spirit I can spot fakes I can discern motives	I believe in the impossible I am confident God will act I know God's will for me I can see God in action	I want to speak for God I have understood tongues I know what God wants to say I hear God's voice
People look to me for clarity I can often see the right path I learn from scripture I read to grow in my faith	People look to me for direction God has used me I have done the impossible I act to grow in my faith	People look to me for sense God has spoken to me I expect interpretations I have asked God to use me
Others see me as wise My prayers help others I long to know more I know I am not wise	I enjoy praying for the sick Healing follows my prayer I feel special when I pray God regularly uses me	I need more words to pray My prayers come from God I am lost for words I have understanding

When all of the boxes have a number, add up the total in each vertical column and place that total in the box provided.

Once this exercise is completed and you have added up the various totals, keep the results safe, for we shall return to them in a later session.

The Body of Christ

One of the diseases of the Western World in our time is the cult of the individual. Sometimes described as the 'stiff upper lip' or the 'John Wayne syndrome,' 'a man's gotta do, what a man's gotta do.' (Could now be even called the 'Die Hard' spirit.) The concept is that we can make it on our own. It is quite impossible to understand the Spiritual Gifts as presented in the Bible if we view our Christianity as an individualistic faith. If we think only about ourselves and our Christian lives, it will lead to significant problems. The Biblical principle of Christian living is that of a corporate society. The gifts which God gives are for the service of others. It is only as we work together and as we share the gifts that God brings that we reveal the Ministry of Jesus in to-days world. If we fail to play our part, however small, the Churches effectiveness greatly suffers.

The Spiritual Gifts.

In the New Testament there are approximately thirty gifts of the Spirit mentioned and while some may argue over which gifts they are and how they overlap, they above all else, reveal the generosity of God. Therefore, the following list must be treated with caution, as it is not exhaustive or set in stone, but it is listed here for your information, prayer and discernment.

List of the Gifts of the Spirit

1. **Word of knowledge** - *to another a message of knowledge by means of the same Spirit (1 Corinthians 12:8 NIV)*
2. **Word of wisdom** - *To one there is given through the Spirit a message of wisdom (1 Corinthians 12:8 NIV)*
3. **Discerning of spirits** - *to another distinguishing between spirits (1 Corinthians 12:10 NIV)*
4. **Faith** - *to another faith by the same Spirit (1 Corinthians 12:9 NIV)*
5. **Gifts of healing** - *to another gifts of healing by that one Spirit (1 Corinthians 12:9 NIV)*
6. **Working of miracles** - *to another miraculous powers ((1 Corinthians 12:10 NIV)*
7. **Prophecy** - *to another prophecy (1 Corinthians 12:10 NIV)*
8. **Tongues** - *to another speaking in different kinds of tongues (1 Corinthians 12:10 NIV)*
9. **Interpretation of tongues** - *and to still another the interpretation of tongues (1 Corinthians 12:10 NIV)*
10. **Deliverance** – *She kept this up for many days. Finally Paul became so annoyed that he turned round and said to the spirit, 'In the name of Jesus Christ I command you to come out of her!' At that moment the spirit left her. (Acts 16:18 NIV)*

11. **Apostleship** - *So Christ himself gave the apostles, (Ephesians 4:11 NIV)*
12. **Evangelism** - *the evangelists (Ephesians 4:11 NIV)*
13. **Teaching** - *and teachers, (Ephesians 4:11 NIV)*
14. **Pastoral guidance** - *the pastors (Ephesians 4:11 NIV)*
15. **Leadership** - *if it is to lead, do it diligently (Romans 12:8 NIV)*
16. **Administration** - *Brothers and sisters, choose seven men from among you who are known to be full of the Spirit and wisdom. We will turn this responsibility over to them (Acts 6:2-3 NIV)*
17. **Ministry/Service** - *if it is serving, then serve; (Romans 12:7 NIV)*
18. **Encouragement/Motivation** - *if it is to encourage, then give encouragement; (Romans 12:8 NIV)*
19. **Intercession** - *In the same way, the Spirit helps us in our weakness. We do not know what we ought to pray for, but the Spirit himself intercedes for us through wordless groans. And he who searches our hearts knows the mind of the Spirit, because the Spirit intercedes for God's people in accordance with the will of God. (Romans 8:26-27 NIV)*
20. **Mercy** - *if it is to show mercy, do it cheerfully. (Romans 12:8 NIV)*
21. **Grace** - *We have different gifts, according to the grace given to each of us. (Romans 12:6 NIV)*
22. **Helping** - *of helping (1 Corinthians 12:28 NIV)*
23. **Giving** - *if it is giving, then give generously; (Romans 12:8 NIV)*
24. **Hospitality** - *Offer hospitality to one another without grumbling. (1 Peter 4:9 NIV)*
25. **Celibacy** - *Now to the unmarried[a] and the widows I say: it is good for them to stay unmarried, as I do. (1 Corinthians 7:8 NIV)*
26. **Missionary** - I became a servant of this gospel by the gift of God's grace given me through the working of his power. (Ephesians 3:7 NIV)
27. **Willingness to face martyrdom** - *If I give all I possess to the poor and give over my body to hardship that I may boast, but do not have love, I gain nothing. (1 Corinthians 13:3 NIV)*
28. **Gift of Voluntary Poverty** - *If I give all I possess to the poor and give over my body to hardship that I may boast, but do not have love, I gain nothing. (1 Corinthians 13:3 NIV)*
29. **The Gift Of Leading Worship** - *Let the message of Christ dwell among you richly as you teach and admonish one another with all wisdom through psalms, hymns, and songs from the Spirit, singing to God with gratitude in your hearts. (Colossians 3:16 NIV)*
30. **Gift of Writing** - *Many have undertaken to draw up an account of the things that have been fulfilled among us, just as they were handed down to us by those who from the first were eye witnesses and servants of the word. With this in mind, since I myself have carefully investigated everything from the beginning, I too decided to write an orderly account for you, most excellent Theophilus, so*

that you may know the certainty of the things you have been taught. (Luke 1:1-4 NIV)

In a previous book in this series where we looked at the reasons the five top reasons why outreach events fail, we considered how people think. These same thought patterns can restrict are acceptance of the gifts that God, the Holy Spirit gives us.

Five struggles that we face when seeking to introduce the gifts of the Holy Spirit into the church.

1. **Apathy**

It is a sad fact that sometimes when we seek to introduce the gifts of the Holy Spirit to a church or fellowship, that those we are hoping to reach are too busy, distracted or do not care about what we are sharing. More often than not they do have a heart for God; actively care for the vulnerable, the lost, the homeless and the victim. But at that actual moment, they are just not interested

2. **Scepticism**

If apathy is not an obstacle, then we may find that having gained their attention that something else is an issue. Some churches do not believe that the gifts of the Holy Spirit are for today, others, either through tradition or restricted practice doubt the gifts are real. Sometimes it is the way we communicate that is at fault. Whatever the reason scepticism becomes a major issue, and the message is ignored.

3. **Relevance**

For others in the church, they may feel that while the gifts of the Spirit are real but they are not for them. They are for the super-Christians, the elite or the chosen ones. Sometimes, the gifts are outside of their sphere of interest, and they ignore them.

4. **Mental barriers**

Sometimes our apathy, scepticism and relevance concerns have been dealt with, but we may have just had an argument with someone, or we do not like the way the message is being presented, and our minds are elsewhere. It can even be they are dwelling on a passage of scripture or worship song. Whatever the reason, these faithful and true disciples are not truly there, and then, despite the leader getting it all right, they still are somewhere else.

5. **Procrastination**

Finally, we are there, in the moment and we have engaged with the fellowship. We are all excited by the possibilities and the vision of what God can do. The apathy, scepticism and relevance issues have been dealt with. We are there in the moment and God the Holy Spirit is moving in power and generosity, all we have to do is respond. We hear God speak, but we remain silent, we know God wants to use us to bring a blessing to others, but we put it off. The truth is, usually when we put something off, we never return to it. The moment has gone and may never return.

Thankfully, when we do dodge the moment and fail to act or pray we discover that God loves those we care for more than we do. Often God will raise someone else to minister to the moment and bring the healing or blessing. It is my hope that this course will so encourage you to take the risk, trust in God and do amazing things.

Actions, Ministries, Gifts and Equipping

In the New Testament, there are four primary listings of Spiritual Gifts. While there are overlapping and the sharing of gifts, they still make four distinctive categories. They are:

a) Actions of the Spirit

These are the gifts which are mainly used within the body of Christ, and they fall into three categories.

Category 1:
Gifts of Revelation
- Words of Wisdom,
- Words of Knowledge
- Discerning of Spirits.

Category 2:
Gifts of Power and Authority
- Gifts of Faith,
- Gifts of Healings,
- The Working of Miracles.

Category 3:
The Gifts of Communication
- The Gift of Prophecy,
- The Gift of Tongues,
- The Interpretation of Tongues.

b) Ministries of the Spirit

The setting aside of Apostles, Prophets, Teachers, Miracles, Gifts of Healings, Gifts of Helping of Administration and of Tongues.

c) Gifts of Grace.

Which includes a prophecy, a service, teaching and exhortation, giving, organising and of mercy.

d) The Equipping of the Saints.

_____
_____
_____
_____
_____
_____

The setting aside of Apostles, Prophets, Evangelists, Pastors and Teachers.

1 Corinthians 12: 1-11

When Paul wrote to the Corinthians, he was concerned they should not be ignorant of the Spiritual Gifts. It is equally important to us today, that we also see a renewal of these gifts in the Church, and that we have a clear understanding of their purpose and place.

A) The Gifts of the Holy Spirit are given by God to enable the members of the Body of Christ to function properly.

B) The Gifts of the Holy Spirit are given by God to enable the active participation of all the members of the Body of Christ.

C) The Gifts of the Holy Spirit represent the bounty of God and are designed to demonstrate within the Body of Christ the beauty of God.

The Word Charisma means gift or present. Charis (Χάρις), often called grace, is the source of every good gift. All the gifts that God gives are out of his Grace, and as a result, they do not represent spiritual maturity in the person who uses that gift, but rather the goodness of God.

Therefore, the gifts of the Holy Spirit, are his Gifts and are therefore given as He chooses. They reveal the presence and working of the Holy Spirit Himself. When we use the gifts, we become a channel for Him to demonstrate Himself in this world. The gifts are given for the benefit of the Church, not an individual. They enable the Church to exercise to Ministry of Jesus. When Paul urges us to, *Now eagerly desire the greater gifts. (1 Corinthians 12.31 NIV)* It is for the benefit of the Church. These spiritual gifts are to be used responsibly and are to be under the control and discipline of the Church. As a result, they are gifts of faith, and if not used in the context of love, the fellowship of believers gains nothing from them.

Setting for the Gifts of the Spirit.

In 1 Corinthians 11 and 12, the context for the use of the Gifts of the Spirit is that of congregational worship.

- 1 Corinthians 11:18

- 1 Corinthians 11:33

- 1 Corinthians 11:20

- 1 Corinthians 12:12
  _____
  _____
  _____
  _____

- 1 Corinthians 12:27
  _____
  _____
  _____
  _____

Using Gifts for Service.
They are gifts given us to use for others. They are developed in the climate of risk-taking and a willingness to fail. They must be developed in an atmosphere where others may be observed exercising the gifts. However, with great power comes great responsibility, or *'...From everyone who has been given much, much will be demanded; and from the one who has been entrusted with much, much more will be asked. (Luke 12.48 NIV)*

Six principles of development
Longer ago than I care to remember, a wise old disciple said these words to me, It is in God's interest that you understand what he is saying to you and that you understand what he wants you to do. Therefore, God will speak to you in circumstances and situations that may be unique to you. However, what you hear will always need to be tested against scripture and be confirmed by other disciples.'

1. **Being open to God.** Be open to God and having a mind that is prepared to learn is important. Sometimes, there is a danger that we have limited God to our expectations. Spiritual, pride, and tradition can prevent us from growing in faith and experience.
2. **Study the Bible.** Beginning with the scripture, investigate the facts about the gifts of the Spirit. In an environment of trust, explore the possibilities scripturally available to you. Importantly, seek to discover the gifts you have, and be prepared to fail and allow others the space to fail too.
3. **Understand your feelings.** Do not be afraid of your feelings, nor be ruled by them. Whatever, your passions, interests and skills allow them to mix with the gifts that you have. It is important that you feel in control and comfortable with your gifts.
4. **Radical honesty.** Be honest with yourself about what has worked and what has not. If something was not successful, admit it and move on. In the same way, if something has worked, then acknowledge it and thank God.
5. **Be prepared to be challenged.** As has been mentioned earlier, the context for the use of the Gifts of the Spirit is in worship. Therefore, allow your fellowship the opportunity to test and confirm your gifts. We are often liable to undervalue our own

contributions and ignore them. Sometimes, the opposite is true, and we need correction. Submission to one another is essential for it allows everything to be tested and establish boundaries.
6. **Be Careful!** With every good gift comes great responsibility. Beware of false pride and arrogance.

As Peter Wagner concludes, '*...every Spiritual Gift we have is a resource which we must use and for which we will be held accountable at the Judgement. Some will have one, some two, and some five. The quantity to begin with does not matter. Stewards are responsible only for what the master has chosen to give them. But the resource that we do have must be used to accomplish the master's purpose.*' *(Your Spiritual Gifts Can Make Your Church Grow, 1979-2012)*

DISCUSSION QUESTIONS:

1. Can you describe a time when you have appreciated someone else's natural gifts?
2. What was the Apostle Paul's attitude towards the gifts of the Holy Spirit? *We have different gifts, according to the grace given to each of us. If your gift is prophesying, then prophesy in accordance with your faith;* [7] *if it is serving, then serve; if it is teaching, then teach;* [8] *if it is to encourage, then give encouragement; if it is giving, then give generously; if it is to lead, do it diligently; if it is to show mercy, do it cheerfully. (Romans 12: 6-8 NIV)*
3. Why do you think the apostle Paul believed that some Christians were ignorant of the Gifts of the Holy Spirit? *Now about the gifts of the Spirit, brothers and sisters, I do not want you to be uninformed. (1 Corinthians 12.1 NIV)*
4. Where do you think the best place to learn how to discover and use the gifts of the Holy Spirit is?
5. If being 'Open to God' is essential, describe a moment in your life when you found yourself skirting around an issue or felt that you have limited what God can do.

Conclusion:

David Pytches in his book, 'Come Holy Spirit,' says '*The Church (Church Cell, such as a Housegroup) is the place to learn to use the gifts and to develop ministries which can then be used in the world to the Glory of God and the extension of God's Kingdom. The meeting place is the learning place for the market place.*'

Many Christians fear that they will not hear God when he is speaking. It is worth remembering that it is in God's interest that we understand what he is saying to us. Therefore, when God, the Holy Spirit speaks and directs us, he will always speak to us in a way that we understand. We should always test what we believe God is saying to us because we all can make mistakes but we should take confidence in the fact that God will speak to and use us.

Reflection on Session 3

- What has God shown me?

- What do I need to ask God for?

- What do I need to do?

- Other comments.

Notes:

SESSION 4
GIFTS OF REVELATION

Knowledge, Wisdom and Discernment
Introduction.

For God to direct his people, it is important that his people hear his voice. Therefore, it is in God's interest that we understand what he is saying. Gifts of Revelation, are the gifts God uses to communicate with his people. These gifts are not to be seen out of the context of scripture, for it is in the Bible that we find the written word of God, and any gift of revelation offered must be tested and not contradict scripture.

With the Biblical safeguard in place there are five principles we should be aware of:

1. The Gifts of the Spirit are given to us to build up the body of Christ and extend the kingdom of God. *Now to each one the manifestation of the Spirit is given for the common good. (1 Corinthians 12.7 NIV)* This is not an academic or theoretical exercise, this is God giving gifts to his church.

2. There are a wide variety of gifts and God gives them to whoever he chooses. *'To one there is given through the Spirit a message of wisdom, to another a message of knowledge by means of the same Spirit,'... 'All these are the work of one and the same Spirit, and he distributes them to each one, just as he determines.' (1 Corinthians 12:8, 11 NIV).*

Notes:

3. The Gifts of the Spirit are given in the context of the body of Christ. A place of risk-taking and possible failure. As a result, they are to be used in a context of love, Paul twice reminds the Corinthians of this.
   1 Corinthians 13.2-3

   _____
   _____
   _____
   _____

4. The gifts are best explored together, in a place of trust and learning. We learn the most when we watch others exercising their gifts and by appreciating the Giver and the gift.
   1 Corinthians 12.27

   _____
   _____
   _____
   _____

5. There is no room for pride or trophy hunting. The gifts are given to build up the church and not to establish a personal badge list or hierarchical positioning. These are gifts of grace for God's church.
   1 Corinthians 12:25-27

   _____
   _____
   _____
   _____

A) Words of Knowledge
Definition: A word of knowledge, is a piece of information learned about a situation or person, given by God as an act of grace and not gained by human understanding or intelligence. It a disclosure of truth, freely given by God to build up the church or to help an individual.

Discussion:
What is the difference between theory, knowledge and experience?

Four types of Knowledge.
1. Human knowledge - that which is acquired through study or practical experience.
2. Spiritual knowledge - that comes from knowing God in Jesus Christ. *Now this is eternal life: that they know you, the only true God, and Jesus Christ, whom you have sent. (John 17:3 NIV)*
3. Word of knowledge - that which comes to the mind of God the Holy Spirit and is shared with us. Information of importance or truth that God would have us know about the past, the present or the future.
4. Fallen supernatural knowledge - that which binds, controls and

enslaves, includes the occult, the psychic and New Age. This knowledge is forbidden by God.

Scriptural Examples of Words of Knowledge.

Old Testament

- **A Warning.**
  2 Kings 6:9-10

- **An encouragement.**
  1 Kings 19:15-18

- **A disclosure of hypocrisy**
  2 Kings 5:25-27a

- **A revelation of where Samuel was hiding.**
  1 Samuel 10:22

- **Insight into someone's thoughts.**
  1 Samuel 9:19

New Testament

- **Foreknowledge and preparation.**
  John 14:29

- **God sends help.**
  Acts 9:11

- **Highlighting corruption in the Church.**
  Acts 5:3

- **Knowledge of people's motivations.**
  John 2:24

- **Humour and provision.**
  Matthew 17:27

- **Preparation for action.**
  Acts 10:19-20
  _____
  _____
  _____
  _____
  _____

- Knowledge of the type of demon troubling a boy.
  Mark 9:25
  _____
  _____
  _____
  _____

How is this Gift Received?

- It is a gift of God. *All these are the work of one and the same Spirit, and he distributes them to each one, just as he determines. (1 Corinthians 12:11 NIV).*
- You may ask for it. *'So I say to you: ask and it will be given to you; seek and you will find; knock and the door will be opened to you. (Luke 11:9 NIV).*
- It may be given to others in the church to help you. *I long to see you so that I may impart to you some spiritual gift to make you strong. (Romans 1:11 NIV)*
- It may have previously been given to you. *For this reason I remind you to fan into flame the gift of God, which is in you through the laying on of my hands. (2 Timothy 1:6 NIV)*
- The Gift is given as a blessing and is not necessarily a permanent gift. *Now to each one the manifestation of the Spirit is given for the common good. (1 Corinthians 12:7 NIV)*

How is this Gift Exercised?

- It is important that such gifts be exercised in the Church and subject to testing.
- Words of knowledge build up the faith of those listening.
- Occasionally, an illustration may be dramatically acted out.
- Multiple words of knowledge may apply to same person or situation.

Notes:
_____
_____
_____
_____
_____
_____
_____
_____
_____
_____

- Words of knowledge can be very precise and accurate to the smallest detail.
- We may be given words of knowledge spontaneously as we wait on God.
- We may feel God's power being with us.
- We may hear a word or expression in our mind.
- We may see an image or a picture.
- We may interpret an image or picture.
- We may sense heat, heaviness or tingling in the hands.
- We may feel unaccustomed pain or stress, a physical feeling in our own body that represents the area that God wants to speak to.
- We must use the Gifts tactfully, with prayer and testing, for the word of God is alive and active. *Sharper than any double-edged sword, it penetrates even to dividing soul and spirit, joints and marrow; it judges the thoughts and attitudes of the heart.* (Hebrews 4:12 NIV)
- Words of knowledge often help us understand the direction in which God is working and what he would have us do.

Notes:

_____
_____
_____
_____
_____
_____
_____
_____
_____
_____
_____
_____
_____
_____
_____
_____
_____

B) Words of Wisdom

Definition: A word of wisdom, is the insight that God gives to the members of the body of Christ to allow the testing and application of a gift of revelation, be that a prophecy or word of knowledge. This wisdom goes beyond human understanding or intelligence, is often for that instant or moment, and helps to bring healing and resolution of a particular need.

Discussion:
What is the difference between theory, wisdom and experience?

There are four types of wisdom:
1. Human Wisdom - that which is acquired through study or practical experience and can aid human development.
   However, it can also become a source of pride, *For it is written: 'I will destroy the wisdom of the wise; the intelligence of the intelligent I will frustrate.' (1 Corinthians 1:19 NIV)*
2. Spiritual Wisdom – that which comes from God and we are encouraged to acquire.
   If any of you lacks wisdom, you should ask God, who gives generously to all without finding fault, and it will be given to you. (James 1:5 NIV)

   but to those whom God has called, both Jews and Greeks, Christ the power of God and the wisdom of God. (1 Corinthians 1:24 NIV).

   For this reason, since the day we heard about you, we have not stopped praying for you. We continually ask God to fill you with the knowledge of his will through all the wisdom and understanding that the Spirit gives. (Colossians 1:9 NIV)
3. Word of Wisdom – the sudden supernatural provision of God's insight into a particular situation, that allows the use exceptional use of a piece of knowledge, either human or divine.
4. Fallen supernatural wisdom - that which binds, controls and enslaves, includes the occult, the psychic and New Age. This knowledge is forbidden by God. *When the woman saw that the fruit of the tree was good for food and pleasing to the eye, and also desirable for gaining wisdom, she took some and ate it. She also gave some to her husband, who was with her, and he ate it. (Genesis 3:6 NIV)*

Scriptural Examples of words of wisdom.

Solomon requested wisdom and was granted it
1Kings 3:12

Jesus promised help to his disciples in the persecutions to

come
Luke 21:15

Jesus demonstrated wisdom when tested:
Matthew 22:18

Mark 2: 27

John 8:7

Matthew 21:24-26

How is this gift applied?

- It is important that such gifts be exercised in the Church, with others and subject to testing. This is particularly true in the context of the healing ministry.
- Words of wisdom are often given spontaneously as we wait on God.
- Words of wisdom often show us how to respond in a difficult situation and may follow a word of Knowledge.
- Words of wisdom build up the faith of those listening.
- We may feel God's power being with us, helping us to speak, pray or act.
- The recipient of the word is being given a direct spiritual revelation and will be able to know its truth immediately. However, caution must be exercised in allowing the recipient time to test and acknowledge this. Never force the issue.
- As in other gifts, wisdom may be expressed in a variety of ways, i.e. Pictures, sounds, feelings, bible passages.
- Occasionally, a word of wisdom may be given as a prophecy.
- Words of wisdom bring glory to God.

It is important that we understand that we are dealing with often difficult and intimate areas of people's lives. A word of wisdom can often be decisive and cut to the heart of an issue. Pastoral sensitivity is vital, and the word of wisdom must be given in a non-judgemental way. If the word is from God, then the recipient will know this and will be given a practical way of dealing with such revelation. However, it takes discernment to recognise whether or not the word is correct. Much can be absorbed by the recipient's reaction to such a word of wisdom.

However, there will be consequences from this divine revelation. The recipient will be blessed, released or given hope. It will build up the faith of those watching and participating.

Notes:

C) The Discerning of Spirits.

Definition: The Discerning of Spirits, is the God given, supernatural ability to know whether something is of God or not. The gift provides insight into the motivation behind words and actions, therefore revealing their human or spiritual origin.

Discussion:
What is the difference between intuition, diagnosis and spiritual discernment?

The use of the Gift.

The importance of testing gifts of revelation. Paul instructs the church to test everything:
1 Thessalonians 5:21

The identification of counterfeits revelations and miracles, exaggerations and lies.
2 Thessalonians 2:9-10

Gifts should be in keeping with the Scripture and God's Church.
1 John 4:6

More than one person at a time can use the gift.
1 Corinthians 14:29

God knows the human heart and reveals the spirit within.
John 1:47

To avoid spiritual 'knockouts!' To prevent a person claiming that they alone have the mind of God.
1 Corinthians 14:32

To the recognise the danger of chaos.

1 Corinthians 14:26-33

In deliverance ministry.

Acts 16:18

To reveal a heart of pride.
1 Corinthian 3:18

For exposing error in believers.
Romans 16:17-18

Discerning when someone is not from God.
Acts 16:16-18

How is this gift applied?

As with all the gifts of the Spirit, the gift of wisdom needs to be shown when exercising discernment. No one person can claim to know the mind of God and a suspected error may be revealed as the discerner's lack of discernment. Therefore it is vital that this gift is used in the context of the church and that the tester is tested. The church should be a place where risks are taken and, in the context of submission to each other and the scripture, gifts exercised.

The human heart is influenced in two main ways, by the Spirit of God and by the spirit of this world. The spirit of this world seeks to destroy God's people and his church, *The thief comes only to steal and kill and destroy; (John 10:10a NIV)*. Whereas the Spirit of God builds up his people and allows them to become more than they are, *I have come that they may have life, and have it to the full. (John 10.10b NIV)*. How all this manifests in people varies from person to person, community to community and church to church. The Church is often attacked at its most weak places, and the gift of discernment is vital to the understanding of God's intentions for us today.

Sometimes it is possible to see someone's intentions via the look in their eyes,

Luke 11:34-35

Other times it can only be seen by the fruit of their behaviour,
Matthew 7:16-20

However, it is always worth remembering that God does not take over a person and force them to speak.
1 Corinthians 14:32

What to do when something disturbing is exposed.

- Trust in God's intentions, the Holy Spirit has revealed something for the benefit of the church and the people involved.
  Romans 8:28

- Do not be afraid or panic!
  1 John 4:18

- Seek God's help, pray and ask for wisdom
  James 1:5

- Trust in God to empower you for the situation.
  Romans 15:13

- Being held accountable, our discernments are bound by our imperfections to make sure you can be responsible by specific trusted people Be ready to hold others accountable, even if that makes you uncomfortable.
  Ephesians 4:1-3

- Seek God's peace, for the absence of peace, is a warning. Peace and confidence comes and grows with prayer. Peace is a gift God that God longs to give, especially in stressful situations.

- Philippians 4:7

Notes:

- Be honest with those you are dealing with and telling them, gently and with compassion, what you are discerning.
- Expect some sort of confirmation or response to help you discern the truth of what you have revealed. Look for an affirmation that their spirit agrees with what you are saying is true.
- If you believe Deliverance Ministry is appropriate, then it may be better to arrange another occasion and venue so that you have the support of the church leadership and that you are covered in prayer.
- If you discern there is a need for exorcism, you must bind the evil spirit in the name of Jesus Christ and seek advice from the leadership of your church. Because of the prevalence of serious mental issues, this area may need external help, support and guidance.
- In all things, give God the glory and thank him for revealing such things to you.

Discussion Questions:

1. Describe a time when you would have liked to receive a gift of revelation.
2. If pastoral sensitivity is vital when the gifts of revelation are offered, can you give examples of good and bad pastoral sensitivity?
3. What do you think the Apostle Paul meant when he wrote these words about the gifts of revelation? *...but test them all; hold on to what is good,' (1 Thessalonians 5:21 NIV)*
4. If the human heart is influenced by the Spirit of God and the spirit of this world. Can you give examples of both and explain how you discerned the difference?
5. Why do you think the apostle Paul had to write these words? *As a prisoner for the Lord, then, I urge you to live a life worthy of the calling you have received. Be completely humble and gentle; be patient, bearing with one another in love. Make every effort to keep the unity of the Spirit through the bond of peace. (Ephesians 4:1-3 NIV)*

Reflection on Session 4

- **What has God shown me?**

  _____
  _____

- **What do I need to ask God for?**

  _____
  _____

- **What do I need to do?**

  _____
  _____

- **Other comments.**

  _____
  _____

SESSION 5
GIFTS OF POWER AND AUTHORITY

Faith, Healing and Miracles

A) Gifts of Faith

Definition: The supernatural certainty from the God the Holy Spirit to a person, or persons, as they face a particular situation, that God is going to act in word or deed. Such confidence is beyond reasonable expectation and can cover both creative blessings and destructive curses.

There are four kinds of faith.

1. **Creedal** – i.e., statements of faith.
   - 1 Corinthians 15:3-4

   - 1 Timothy 2:5-6

   - Philippians 2.6-11

   - Jude 3:24-25

2. **Saving faith** – that comes from knowing God in Jesus Christ
   - John 3:16

   - Ephesians 2:8

   - Hebrews 11:1-4

   - Hebrews 11:6

3. **The gift of Faith** – given by God the Holy

Spirit to an individual at a particular time

- Matthew 17:20 _____

- Matthew 21:21 _____

- 1 Corinthians 13:2 _____

Scriptural Examples of the Gift of Faith

- Family blessings - Hebrews 11:20-21 _____

- Protection – Daniel 6.16 _____

- Healing – Acts 28:5 _____

- Provision – 1 Kings 17:5-6 _____

4. **Faith as a fruit of the Spirit**
- Galatians 5:22 _____

- Raising the dead – 1 Kings 17:23 _____

- Resistance to error - Luke 4:4 _____

- Avoiding temptation - Matthew 4:10 _____

- God promises we will

- not be overtaken with temptation –

  1 Corinthians 10:13

- God will keep us from falling –
  Jude 24-25

- Victory over death –
  Acts 2:32

- All things will work for good –
  Romans 8.28

Faith builds up the church

- Bringing glory to God –
  John 14.13

- Encouraging the disciples –
  Matthew 21:20

- Promotes new faith –
  John 11:45

- Builds the Church –
  Acts 20.32

Conclusion

The gift of faith is the foundation for all the gifts of power and authority. Without it, the church would not have the confidence to act and proclaim. The gift of faith often goes unseen and is less spectacular than other gifts of power and authority. However, the gift often achieves its outcomes because it works silently and discretely behind the scenes.

Notes:

B) Gifts of Healings

Definition – A supernatural gift that is channelled through the church to bring a variety of kinds of healing and restoration to individuals in need through the power of the Holy Spirit.

'Christian healing is, first and foremost, about Christ. It follows the pattern he set in his own ministry, and the commission he gave to his disciples, and the fact that it happens at all is the fruit of his work, both in the creation and in the salvation of mankind. In both these mighty works, humankind has been created and re-created in the image of God — has been made whole. This is what distinguishes Christian healing from other types of healing. It is the whole work of Christ, in a person's body, mind and spirit, designed to bring that person to that wholeness which is God's will for us all.' (Bishop Maddox: Twenty Questions about Healing)

There are four types of healing:

1. **Human Healing** - that which is acquired through study or practical experience and can aid human development. It includes everything developed by the medical and caring professions.
2. **Spiritual Healing** – that which comes from the supernatural power of God.
   In co-operation with the medical and caring professions
   Luke 5:14

   _____
   _____
   _____

3. **Fallen supernatural healing** - that which binds, controls and enslaves, includes the occult, the psychic and New Age.
4. **False healing** – that which is an illusion, a slight of the hand, a confidence trick to obtain money, fame or influence.

General Comments

The growth in the healing ministry has been a mark of the influence of the renewal movement on the church as a whole. It is now a ministry that can be exercised in a variety of places and ways, as part of public healing services, in house groups, fellowships and in small groups. In fact wherever and whenever Christian gather to meet and pray. With this growing popularity, it is worth reminding ourselves of the foundations for the gifts of healing.

1. It comes from God and is a result of the sacrifice Jesus made for us.
   - Matthew 8: 16-17

   _____
   _____
   _____
   _____

   - 1 Peter 2:24

   _____
   _____
   _____
   _____

2. The Gifts of Healing comes from God, the Holy Spirit –
   1 Corinthians 12:9

   _____
   _____
   _____
   _____

3. The gift of healing does not work in isolation from the other spiritual gift such as words of knowledge, wisdom, discernment, faith and miracles.

4. We are copying the actions and ministry of Jesus
   John 5:19

   _____
   _____
   _____

5. The gift of healing is not in itself a sign of the disciple's maturity and care must be taken not to let pride take hold.
   Philippians 2:1-4

6. _____
   _____
   _____
   _____
   _____

'The healing ministry is one of the greatest opportunities the Church has today for sharing the gospel. More than before in the last hundred years, many in our society realise there is a spiritual as well as a physical and a mental dimension to healthy living. 'Wholeness' is the in-word: it is what everyone longs for...' (A Time to Heal: The Development of Good Practice in the Healing Ministry: A Handbook)

The Purpose of Healing

When Jesus commissioned his disciples, he sent them out with the instruction to heal the sick and proclaim the good news of the Kingdom of God. In doing so, Jesus linked healing and wholeness with the Kingdom of God. It is through the healing ministry of the church that Jesus meets us at our point of need. This healing covers every area of suffering that impacts our human existence, and nothing is excluded.

- Matthew 4:23
  _____
  _____
  _____
  _____

- Matthew 9:35
  _____
  _____
  _____
  _____

- Matthew 10:7
  _____
  _____
  _____
  _____

- Luke 9:2
  _____
  _____
  _____
  _____

- Luke 9:11
  _____
  _____
  _____
  _____

- Luke 10:9
  _____
  _____

Therefore, the healing ministry of the church is intended:
- To help people find salvation.
- To be a sign of God's love for the world.
- To begin the process of wholeness to a person's life.
- To bring healing or to alleviate the hold of memories
- To release feelings and emotions
- To bring forgiveness and hope to the soul
- To alleviate physical and mental suffering
- To build up the faith of the church
- To bring glory to God

Practical Matters for Ministry

You are entering the realm of spiritual warfare, and any who engage in healing will face spiritual conflict. This conflict can be persistent and will have the aim of undermining what you are doing and will attempt to distract you from giving glory to God.

During Preparation

- Unexpected feelings of depression.
- The desire to run away and hide.
- A sense of dislocation and separation.
- Unexpected tiredness
- and feelings of isolation.
- Lack of interest in what's going on.
- The sense of unworthiness.
- Lack of peace and an onset of frustration.

- Tension or anger with another person close by.
- An unexpected incident drags your attention away.

During Ministry:
Often the following can be summed up as a list of temptations.
- Diversions and tangents.
- Doubt that God is going to do anything.
- Dwelling on the negative - nothing is happening.
- Unwholesome thoughts.
- The temptation to force the moment.
- The temptation to stop listening to God.
- Confusion and disinterest.
- Uncertainty.
- The desire to finish quickly.

After Ministry:
These feelings are not limited to the healing ministry.
- The frustration that nothing appeared to happen – after nothing visible has happened.
- A feeling of failure
- Depression and a sense of unworthiness.
- Overwhelming tiredness.
- Confusion and mixed emotions.
- Doubting what happened was real – after something positive has happened.
- The temptation to pride.
- Failing to give the glory and thanks to God.
- To forget what happened.

Notes:

The setting for Ministry of Healing
The ministry of healing comes in the context of the church, it can be the church 'sent-out' or the church 'in worship', it honours Jesus and is a blessing of God. *Is anyone among you in trouble? Let them pray. Is anyone happy? Let them sing songs of praise. Is anyone among you ill? Let them call the elders of the church to pray over them and anoint them with oil in the name of the Lord. And the prayer offered in faith will make the sick person well; the Lord will raise them up. If they have sinned, they will be forgiven. Therefore confess your sins to each other and pray for each other so that you may be healed. The prayer of a righteous person is powerful and effective. (James 5:13-16 NIV)*

We begin by asking the Father to give us the Holy Spirit to us. *If you then, though you are evil, know how to give good gifts to your children, how much more will your Father in heaven give the Holy Spirit to those who ask him!' (Luke 13:11 NIV)*

Ministry begins with an invitation for God to fill his church with the Holy Spirit and to bless his people. Healing comes out of a loving relationship with God. Therefore, we need to:
- Invite and honour the Holy Spirit.

What to expect practically.
There are vast varieties of ways that God can indicate to you that he wants to do something extraordinary:
- A sudden feeling of compassion for a person.
- An unexpected 'knowing' that God wants to act.
- A feeling of power. Some people have described their hands as tingling or feeling warm.
- Other gifts of the Spirit are used, gifts of Faith, Knowledge, Wisdom and Discernment.
- A sense that God is in control and that we can trust him to act through us.
- You are given inspired thoughts, pictures or impressions.
- You may even imagine or envision a picture of the healing miracle happening.
- Scripture verses spring into mind.
- You feel an unexpected pain indicating an area God wants to heal or improve.
- It may even be the description of a symptom.

Further considerations
- When healing takes place, it is the action of God, and all the glory

is his. It is easy to become proud when God uses us.
- When spiritual warfare is involved, we must give ourselves to God and resist the devil. *Submit yourselves, then, to God. Resist the devil, and he will flee from you. (James 4.7 NIV)*
- There are 'times and seasons' for God's gifts, we need to learn to live in God's tides.
- While God may give someone a gift of healing for a particular occasion, sometimes he gives others a ministry of healing.
- As our faith and trust in God grow so does the frequency that God will give us his gifts.
- God may choose you to receive any gift, but he may also develop in you a ministry in a particular gift. When this happens, it is vital that we do not let pride overcome us and that we walk humbly with our God.
- Occasionally, God will give somebody a specific ministry in one particular area of healing.
- Never rely on your own emotions or feelings, just because you felt nothing happened does not mean that healing did not take place.
- Test everything.
- Sometimes God acts independently of us and whatever we do will bring healings.
- Be humble and gracious, and give all the glory to God.

The wider implications...
The gift of God's healing can happen instantly or swiftly, but often healing is a continuing process, taking the time to bring deep restoration the whole person. We need to recognise this and take into consideration the ongoing pastoral care and spiritual development of the people involved. Often that may mean observing the connection with the medical and caring professions.

Notes:

C) The Gift of Working Miracles.

Definition
The gift of working miracles is the supernatural gift that God, the Holy Spirit, gives to intervene in the natural order of the universe for the advancement of his kingdom and people.

There are three types of miracles:
1. **God given miracles** – that which comes from the supernatural power of God.
2. **Fallen supernatural miracles** - that which binds, controls and enslaves, includes the occult, the psychic and New Age.
3. **False miracles** – that which is an illusion, a slight of the hand, a confidence trick to obtain money, fame or influence.

Biblical examples:
There vast amounts of accounts of miracles in the scriptures, these are just a random selection from the Old and New Testaments:

To reveal God's power.
- Psalm 77.14 NIV

- 1 Kings 1837-39

- Job 5:9

- Jeremiah 32:21

- The apostles – Acts 2:43

- To Stephen – Acts 6:8

To confirm the word preached
- To support Moses – Exodus 7:3

To provide for those in need.
- Manna in the desert – Exodus 16:35

The Holy Spirit Course: More Than Just Words

- Elijah is fed by ravens – 1 Kings 17:6

To rescue or comfort God's people.
- Moses parts the Red Sea Exodus 14:16

- Jesus calms the storm - Mark 4:39

- Peter escapes with an angel's help from prison Acts 12:8-10

To raise the dead.
- Elisha and the widow's son - 2 Kings 4:32-35

- Jesus raises the dead - John 11.43-44

To exercise God's judgement.
- In the Psalms – Psalm 105.5

- Ananias and Sapphira - Acts 5:5

Introduction to the gift.
- A miracle is a temporary supernatural interruption in the natural order of the universe for the advancement of his kingdom and people.
- The majority of Jesus' miracles came out of acts of compassion.
- All gifts of healing are miracles.
- Christians are told to expect 'signs and wonders.'
- The persecuted church often testifies to experiencing this gift.
- Miracles and science are not in contradiction.

How we ask for a gift of miracles will vary according to the situation that we are in. We are encouraged by Jesus to ask for what we need:
'So I say to you: ask and it will be given to you; seek and you will find; knock and the door will be opened to you. For everyone who asks receives; the one who seeks finds; and

to the one who knocks, the door will be opened. (Luke 11:9-10 NIV)
So while we cannot demand a miracle, God may be generous and give one to us, and he may even allow us to help others in need. Often such miracles come out of a profound sense of anger, danger or compassion and their outcomes, as well providing for a particular need, bring glory to God. As with the gift of healing, other gifts will be evident, such as gifts of faith, knowledge and wisdom.

Responses to the Gift of Miracles.
It will bring glory to God.
It will build up the kingdom of God.
It will rescue from or alleviate the disciple from danger.
It will lead people to Christ.
It will build up the church and affirm God's love for it.

Discussion Questions:

1. Why do you think the gift of faith is so important to the church?
2. Confidentiality and respect are key characteristics of Christian ministry. Can you describe a time when it would be inappropriate share publically God's healing?
3. Gifts of power and authority can be exciting, can you think of a time when you have caused a problem by being over exuberant?
4. Sometimes our scars are on the inside, and we struggle to share them. Can you describe a time when you felt unable to share those scars and what impact that had on you not talking about them?
5. Sometimes it seems that some people find healing and others do not. Can you think of an occasion when you have said, 'That's not fair' and discuss how that has affected you?

Reflection on Session 5

- **What has God shown me?**

  _____
  _____

- **What do I need to ask God for?**

  _____
  _____

- **What do I need to do?**

- **Other comments.**

Notes:

SESSION 6
GIFTS OF COMMUNICATION

Prophecy, Tongues and Interpretation of Tongues

A) The Gift of Prophecy

Definition
The Gift of Prophecy is a spontaneous message, usually in human words, given as a unique ability to the Body of Christ, based on a personal revelation from the Holy Spirit for the purpose of encouragement, challenge, enlightenment, encouragement, comfort, reprimand, conviction or direction.

- *to another miraculous powers, to another prophecy, to another distinguishing between spirits, to another speaking in different kinds of tongues, and to still another the interpretation of tongues. (1 Corinthians 12.10 NIV)*
- *Follow the way of love and eagerly desire gifts of the Spirit, especially prophecy. (1 Corinthians 14:1 NIV)*

Four types of prophecy.
1. **Forthtelling,** to make public, someone who preaches something actively, in a forthright fashion, presenting the truth of a matter, as in teaching and evangelism
2. **Foretelling** or prediction of what is to come. To foretell the future as in the books of Daniel and Revelation.
3. **The words of a prophet**, divinely inspired utterance or revelation: but not automatically free from human error, and therefore needing testing by Scripture and those with mature spiritual wisdom, or those with the gift of Discernment.
4. **Fallen supernatural prediction**- that which binds, controls and enslaves, includes the occult, fortune telling, horoscopes, the psychic and New Age.

It is worth noting that the gift of prophecy is open to all believers although some may develop a ministry of prophecy.

- *'And afterwards, I will pour out my Spirit on all people. Your sons and daughters will prophesy, your old men will dream dreams, your young men will see visions. (Joel 2:28 NIV)*
- *So Christ himself gave the apostles, the prophets, the evangelists, the pastors and teachers, (Ephesians 4:11 NIV)*

The Purpose of Prophecy

- **It builds up the church**
  1 Corinthians 14:3

- **A sign for unbelievers**
  1 Corinthians 14:24-25

- **Prophecy is not the equivalent of Scripture**
  1 Corinthians 14:32

  This gift may also be used to foretell or predict, but subject to this warning
  Deuteronomy 18:20-22

- **Not all prophecy is irrevocable**
  Jeremiah 18:7-8

- **The importance of speaking out**
  Ezekiel 33:6

A) The Gift of Prophecy

The primary setting for prophecy is in worship. However, a word may come to an individual but it always for the benefit of the Church.
  1 Corinthians 14.26

The Exercise of Prophecy.

- **The gift of Prophecy is a gift of God,** and he gives it to whomever he wills
  1 Corinthians 12:11

-

- **Eagerly desire the gifts of God**
  1 Corinthians 14.1

- **The primary setting for prophecy is in worship and adoration**
  Acts 13:2

- **It should be restricted to two or three at one time**
  1 Corinthians 14:29-33

- **The one prophesying should always be fully in control of themselves**
  1 Corinthians 14:3

- **Be prepared to speak out** – You may have to show courage to speak out
  1 Corinthians 14:26

Acts 2:17-18

- **Be humble and not proud**
  1 Thessalonians 5:19-21

- **Thank God when he uses you and when he uses others**
  1 Thessalonians 5:18

- Recognise that not all will become prophets.

Practical suggestions

- When you gather for worship expect God to speak - *What then shall we say, brothers and sisters? When you come together, each of you has a hymn, or a word of instruction, a revelation, a tongue or an interpretation. Everything must be done so that the church may be built up (1 Corinthians 14:26 NIV)*
- Prophecy may be expressed in a variety of ways – a picture, an action, a word uttered loudly or quietly, in a song, in the choice of a verse of scripture.
- You may feel nervous or slightly excited before you speak.
- If two or three have already spoken, you may write your prophecy down or offer it on another occasion.
- You may only know the beginning of what you want to say, you may be given more as you speak. Sometimes the prophecy will be shared between a few people.

- If you are slow to speak out, you may hear someone else express the prophecy that you were given.
- The Lord may give you an individual word of prophecy when you are praying on your own, but you will have to wait for the prophecy to be tested.

Response to Prophecy

- **All prophecy should be tested**
  1 Corinthians 14:29

- **The prophecy should be tested against Scripture**
  2 Peter 1:20

- **The person giving the prophecy must be of good character**
  Matthew 7:16

1 Corinthians 14:32

- Is the prophecy in line with what God is already doing?
- **The prophecy should build up the church**
  1 Corinthians 14.26b
-

- The gift of discernment should be used to test it.
- A summary should be given at the end of any time of prophecy.

Notes:

B) The Gift of Tongues.

Of all the gifts of the Holy Spirit the 'gift of tongues' is one of the most debated and misunderstood. Many Christians are not familiar with speaking in tongues and find the concept, strange, awkward or embarrassing. The early church was given the ability to speak in tongues, and its first occurrence is described fully in Acts 2. Filled with the Holy Spirit, the disciples began to speak in the languages of all the pilgrims visiting Jerusalem, and many came to faith because of it. Eventually, the excitement of speaking tongues caused the Apostle Paul to have to write about it and give the disciples a set of instructions. I Corinthians 14 describe the chaos and Paul's suggestions for their use in public worship.

Definition.

The gift of speaking in Tongues is the use of spontaneously inspired words spoken using the natural human voice. The languages spoken, or sung, are recited without the use of the conscious mind and are completely unlearned by the speaker.

Biblical background

In Mark's gospel when Jesus gave the disciples the great commission he told them -, *And these signs will accompany those who believe: in my name they will drive out demons; they will speak in new tongues; (Mark 16:17 NIV)* This we see fulfilled in the book of Acts and in the writings of the Apostle Paul.
In 1 Corinthians 14 Paul instructs the church on the proper use of the gift:

- **It is a legitimate gift of communication from the Holy Spirit.** The gift happens when the believer permits the Holy Spirit to guide the words they speak
  1 Corinthians 14:2
  _____
  _____
  _____
  _____

- **It helps build up the believer's prayer life.** This is the only gift of the Spirit which the Christian believer can use for their own personal growth and development
  1 Corinthians 14:4
  _____
  _____
  _____

- **We are all encouraged to seek the gift, though not everyone receives it**
  1 Corinthians 14:5
  _____
  _____
  _____

- **Praying and singing in tongues should be**

mixed with praying and singing with the mind
1 Corinthians 14:15

- No more than two or three may speak in tongues at once
  1 Corinthians 14:27

- There must be an interpretation of the gift
  1 Corinthians 14:28

- The gift should be tested
  1 Corinthians 14:29

- The gift can confuse non-believers
  1 Corinthians 14:23

- Tongues should not be forced upon anyone
  1 Corinthians 12:30

- Do not prevent people from speaking in tongues
  1 Corinthians 14:39-40

Notes:

Types of Tongues.
- **Human language**, that is unknown to the speaker but is understood by the person whose language it is
  Acts 2:4-8
  _____
  _____
  _____
  _____

- **The language of angels,** that is unknown on earth but needs interpretation
  1 Corinthians 13: 1
  _____
  _____

- **Tongues in public worship**, but need interpretation
  1 Corinthians 14:26-28
  _____
  _____
  _____

- **The use of tongues in private**
  1 Corinthians 14:4
  _____
  _____
  _____
  _____
  _____
  _____

The Purpose of Tongues.
- A sign to unbelievers when it is understood by an unbelieving bystander.
- To build up the body of Christ using all its members
- Public or private edification
- A language of love
- Builds up an individual's prayer life
- It allows the believer to pray when their words have run out
  Romans 8:26
  _____
  _____
  _____

- It is a means of prayer and intercession.
- It is used in spiritual warfare and cannot be opposed
- It is empowering, refreshing and uplifting
- It is also effective in praying for revival.
- It can be used when praying for other gifts of the Holy Spirit.

Helpful guidelines to the gift of Tongues
Great care must be exercised in public worship when a tongue is used. Tongues can often be a catalyst for worship and the other gifts, and it is

easy to blend them together. When someone has given a tongue then an interpretation is required. However, this interpretation can be confused with a subsequent prophecy, a word of knowledge or wisdom. When this happens, the leader should return to the tongue and seek an interpretation. More often than not, a tongue in public worship is an outburst of praise that offers glory to God. This is helpful, for it lifts our spirits into God's presence and distinguishes the tongue from the other gifts of communication.

Receiving the Gift.

There is no one way of receiving this gift, but as in all the gifts of the Holy Spirit, it often is given after we asked for it.

- It often follows after we have asked to be filled with the Holy Spirit.
- It is easier to use the gift for the first time during a song rather than speaking out loud.
- It is not a gift that can be forced. Instead, it is wise to wait on God - *but those who hope in the LORD will renew their strength. They will soar on wings like eagles; they will run and not grow weary, they will walk and not be faint. (Isaiah 40:31 NIV)*
- It is often helpful to be prayed for by others.
- Once the gift is given, it is used on our side by an act of will.

Responses to Tongues.

- When used in public there should always be an explanation of what the gift is for anyone new to the gift.
- No more than three individual tongues at once in the meeting.
- There should be time given for interpretation.
- All may pray for the interpretation when a tongue is given, including the person who had the tongue.
- There are different types of tongues, so discernment is required.
- Everything should be done in an orderly way.

Notes:

_____
_____
_____
_____
_____
_____
_____
_____

C) The Interpretation of Tongues.

Definition
This gift is a supernatural revelation from the Holy Spirit that allows the listener to interpret the spontaneously inspired words spoken in tongues. The words received are a dynamic equivalent rather than a word for word translation of the gift of tongues. The interpretation of the tongue in public worship is usually an outburst of praise that offers glory to God.

Introduction:
- The gift of interpretation comes from the mind of God.
- The gift of interpretation is as much a gift of the Spirit as the utterance.
- The interpreter receives a dynamic equivalent rather than a word for word translation.
- You may feel nervous or slightly excited before you speak.
- If two or three have already spoken, you may write your interpretation down or offer it on another occasion.
- You may only know the beginning of what you want to say, you may be given more as you speak. Sometimes the interpretation will be shared between a few people.
- If you are slow to speak out, you may hear someone else express the interpretation that you were given.

The purpose of the Gift:
- To bring praise to God.
- To give the believer words when their own words fail.
- To build up the church by bringing understanding and insight.

Exercise of the Gift
- The interpretation may come through pictures, symbols or words.
- The gift of Faith is needed for interpretation.

- Notes:

Notes:

- The Gift of Discernment is required to confirm the interpretation.
- All those who speak in tongues should pray for interpretation.
- As the interpretation is a dynamic equivalent, the length of responding may not correspond to the time spent speaking in tongues.
- Nerves may make the initial interpretation less clear, be prepared to be an active listener.
- A right relationship with God and the body of Christ is essential.
- There should be an interpretation of every tongue.
- There must be no rivalry among interpreters.
- No more than three tongues and interpretations at one time.
- No interpretation may go beyond scripture.

Discussion Questions:

1. What do you think the Apostle Paul meant when he wrote these words? *Follow the way of love and eagerly desire gifts of the Spirit, especially prophecy. (1 Corinthians 14:1 NIV)*
2. When you gather for worship, do you expect God to speak to you? How do you think we can put these words of the Apostle Paul into action. *What then shall we say, brothers and sisters? When you come together, each of you has a hymn, or a word of instruction, a revelation, a tongue or an interpretation. Everything must be done so that the church may be built up (1 Corinthians 14:26 NIV)*
3. Many Christians are not familiar with speaking in tongues and find the concept, strange, awkward or embarrassing. What place do you think the speaking of tongues has in the church today?
4. Describe an occasion when words have run out, and you have not known what to pray
5. Why do you think that a right relationship with God and the body of Christ is essential when asking for gifts of communication?

Reflection on Session 6

- **What has God shown me?**

- **What do I need to ask God for?**

- **What do I need to do?**

- **Other comments.**

SESSION 7
THE GIFTS IN WORSHIP AND THE PRAYER OF BOLDNESS

Introduction to the Open to God Sessions
In Chapters 1-6 we considered God the Holy Spirit in the Old and New Testaments and have looked at the following sections:
- Who is the Holy Spirit?
- The Holy Spirit and You
- Introducing the Gifts of the Spirit
- Gifts of Revelation
    - Words of Knowledge
    - Words of Wisdom
    - Discerning of Spirits
- Gifts of Power and Authority
    - Gifts of Faith
    - Gifts of Healings
    - The working of Miracles
- Gifts of Communication
    - The Gift of Prophecy
    - The Gift of Tongues
    - The Interpretation of Tongues

The next three chapters are of a more practical nature, and they would be best considered in the context of prayer and worship.

Worship
'Christian worship is the most momentous, the most urgent, the most glorious action that can take place in human life' (Karl Barth)

Worship is the expression of feeling, or will, of reverence and adoration for God. It is the place where we willingly submit ourselves to the influence and direction of God, the Holy Spirit. It is, therefore, no surprise that when we gather in the name of Jesus and seek to worship him in Spirit and truth that we find ourselves receiving the grace and giftings of God.

Consider the following scriptures:
- John 4:24
- Romans 12:1

- Acts 13:2
  _____
  _____
  _____
  _____
  _____
  _____
  _____
  _____
  _____
  _____

- 1 Corinthians 14:26
  _____
  _____
  _____
  _____

- James 5:13-16
  _____
  _____
  _____
  _____

Practicalities

In these Open to God sessions, we intend to wait on God and receive his gifts and blessings, but it does beg the question:
- How mature does a Christian person need to be to receive such benefits?

The answer is quite simple:
- We need to be like the disciples!

If you study the gospels and the book of Acts you will discover that the disciples were:
- Quarrelsome
- Faint-hearted
- Critical
- Deceived
- Weak
- Gloomy
- Slow to learn
- Cynical
- Disloyal
- Ambitious
- Unforgiving
- Difficult
- Unloving
- Judgemental

That is quite a list, and these were the people Jesus appointed to go out in his name and build his church. However, that is not to say these are the attributes we need or want to see in worship, they are not! They do, however; put us in good company and can assure us that God can use us also.

The Apostle Paul urges us to order our worship in a way that brings glory to God:
- 1 Corinthians 14:40

  _____
  _____
  _____

- Colossians 2:5

  _____
  _____
  _____

We can also be encouraged by the words of James quoted above when he states
- *The prayer of a righteous person is powerful and effective. (James 5:16b NIV)*

Now it is easy, I admit, to look at that verse and, after a hard and honest look at oneself, to believe that explains why our prayers are so weak. On close examination, we may believe that we are not righteous, and indeed that is true
- Romans 3:23

  _____
  _____

However, we have been made perfect, righteous and holy:
- Hebrews 10:14

  _____
  _____

- Hebrews 12:23

  _____
  _____

- 1 Corinthians 15:57

  _____
  _____

Therefore, if we have been made righteous by the redeeming love of the Lord Jesus Christ and we have been filled with the Holy Spirit, then our prayers too will be powerful and effective. Take heart, God can use you!

Practical Considerations

- **Being open to God.** Be open to God and having a mind that is prepared to learn is important. Sometimes, there is a danger that we have limited God to our expectations. Spiritual, pride, and tradition can prevent us from growing in faith and experience.
- **Study the Bible.** Beginning with the scripture, investigate the facts about the gifts of the Spirit. In an environment of trust, explore the possibilities scripturally available to you. Importantly, seek to discover the gifts you have, and be prepared to fail and allow others the space to fail too.
- **Understand your feelings.** Do not be afraid of your feelings, nor be ruled by them. Whatever, your passions, interests and skills allow them to mix with the gifts that you have. It is important that you feel in control and comfortable with your gifts.
- **Radical honesty.** Be honest with yourself about what has worked and what has not. If something was not successful, admit it and move on. In the same way, if something has worked, then acknowledge it and thank God.
- **Be prepared to be challenged.** As has been mentioned earlier, the context for the use of the Gifts of the Spirit is in worship. Therefore, allow your fellowship the opportunity to test and confirm your gifts. We are often liable to undervalue our own contributions and ignore them. Sometimes, the opposite is true, and we need correction. Submission to one another is essential for it allows everything to be tested and establish boundaries.
- **Be Careful!** With every good gift comes great responsibility. Beware of false pride and arrogance.

As mentioned in the earlier sessions expect the following:

During Preparation
- Unexpected feelings of depression.
- The desire to run away and hide.
- A sense of dislocation and separation.
- Unexpected tiredness and feelings of isolation.
- Lack of interest in what's going on.
- The sense of unworthiness.
- Lack of peace and an onset of frustration.
- Tension or anger with another person close by.
- An unexpected incident drags your attention away.

During Ministry:
Often the following can be summed up as a list of temptations.
- Diversions and tangents.
- Doubt that God is going to do anything.
- Dwelling on the negative - nothing is happening.
- Unwholesome thoughts.
- The temptation to force the moment.
- The temptation to stop listening to God.
- Confusion and disinterest.
- Uncertainty.
- The desire to finish quickly.

After Ministry:
These feelings are not limited to the healing ministry.
- The frustration that nothing appeared to happen – after nothing visible has happened.
- A feeling of failure
- Depression and a sense of unworthiness.
- Overwhelming tiredness.
- Confusion and mixed emotions.
- Doubting what happened was real – after something positive has happened.
- The temptation to pride.
- Failing to give the glory and thanks to God.
- To forget what happened.

Open to God 1

Begin with prayer and worship and invite God the Holy Spirit to come upon you and ask the Holy Spirit to give you his gifts. It is also important that everything is done in a relaxed but reverent atmosphere, providing space for people to wait on God and to take risks. Risk taking should be done in a context of love and community. Finally, it is essential that you all agree on the principle of radical honesty, that no matter how unusual, odd or strange and impression you get of God speaking that you will share it with the group and that if the message is for you, you will own it publically. For this to work there has to be an agreement of trust, that what is said in the session stays in the session and that if the revelation is deeply private, that that privacy is respected and protected.

Bible Study

Please look at the Disciples prayer in **Acts 4:13-31** and ask the group or groups to answer these questions:
- What do we learn about God the Holy Spirit?
- What do we learn about how to pray?
- What should we ask for in our prayer?

Please use what you have learnt in your Bible Study to help you to pray and wait on God. Remember to invite God, the Holy Spirit to come upon you and move in power.

Time of Waiting
- Allow at least forty minutes for God to act and speak.
- If your group finds it helpful, play some quite worshipful music.
- Provide pens, paper and other creative items.

Time of Reflection
- Thank God in advance for speaking
- Share your thoughts, images, pictures
- Ask God to reveal if they are for you
- Give the glory to God
- Close in prayer
- Allow spiritual digestion time

Discussion Questions:

1. Are these words of Karl Barth true in your experience? *'Christian worship is the most momentous, the most urgent, the most glorious action that can take place in human life' (Karl Barth)* If not how do we make our worship more inspiring?
2. How do you think we can put these words of Jesus into action? *God is spirit, and his worshippers must worship in the Spirit and in truth.' (John 4:24 NIV)*
3. Give an example of when you have gathered for worship and had unexpected feelings of depression and wanted to run away and hide.
4. Have you ever doubted that something was real after something positive in worship has happened? Why do you think you felt this way?
5. A core principle of this course is that it is essential that we all

agree on the principle of radical honesty. Discuss how this principle makes you feel and what it tells you about yourself.

Notes:

Reflection on Session 7

- **What has God shown me?**

- **What do I need to ask God for?**

- **What do I need to do?**

SESSION 8
THE GIFTS IN ACTION

Open To God 2

'If we are to see a major move of God in our nation then that work will begin in individual lives. If we are to challenge our society with the good news of the Jesus they reject then we must find a new power from outside ourselves. That power rests with God himself.

To some of us the call will come simply to humble ourselves and pray; others will need to seek ministry and help. The end result is the same lives filled and renewed by the Spirit of God. Then, and only then, will people recognise what they saw in those early disciples the life of Jesus reflected in his people.' (Clive Calver - The Holy Spirit)

Ask Jesus to fill you with his Holy Spirit. If he assures you in your heart that he has done that already then keep going! If you have any doubts consider these passages:

- **Offer yourself to God**
  Romans 12:1-2

- **Ask God to fill you with the Holy Spirit**
  Luke 11:9-10

  Luke 11:13

- **Give yourself to God in obedience**
  Acts 5.32

- **Have faith in God**
  Galatians 3:2

  _____
  _____
  _____
  _____

Begin with prayer and worship and invite God the Holy Spirit to come upon you and ask the Holy Spirit to give you his gifts. It is also important that everything is done in a relaxed but reverent atmosphere, providing space for people to wait on God and to take risks. Risk taking should be done in a context of love and community. Finally, it is essential that you all agree on the principle of radical honesty, that no matter how unusual, odd or strange and impression you get of God speaking that you will share it with the group and that if the message is for you, you will own it publically. For this to work there has to be an agreement of trust, that what is said in the session stays in the session and that if the revelation is deeply private, that that privacy is respected and protected.

Bible Study

Please look at the words of the Apostle Paul in **1 Corinthians 14** and ask the group or groups to answer these questions:
- What do we learn about God the Holy Spirit?
- What are we encouraged by Paul to do?
- Which spiritual gifts would you like to have?
- Why should everything be done in a fitting and orderly way?

Comment:

1 Timothy 2:11 (NIVUK)

11 A woman should learn in quietness and full submission.

Galatians 3:28 There is neither Jew nor Gentile, neither slave nor free, nor is there male and female, for you are all one in Christ Jesus.
Please use what you have learnt in your Bible Study to help you to pray and wait on God. Remember to invite God, the Holy Spirit to come upon you and move in power.

Time of Waiting
- Allow at least forty minutes for God to act and speak.
- If your group finds it helpful, play some quite worshipful music.
- Provide pens, paper and other creative items.

Time of Reflection
- Thank God in advance for speaking
- Share your thoughts, images, pictures
- Ask God to reveal if they are for you
- Give the glory to God
- Close in prayer
- Allow spiritual digestion time

Accompanying, this book there is a Resource Booklet that contains eighteen images randomly selected to be used in Session 8 of this ten-week course. Seven of which pictures have been included in this book. The concept behind the use of these images is simple. In small groups of twos or threes, each person in the group selects a picture and prays, meditates and reflects over the image. After this extended period, in an atmosphere of love and fellowship, each person then shares what they believe God, the Holy Spirit is saying to the other people in their group. These thoughts are then prayed over and tested in an attitude of radical honesty. Above all, this should be done gently and in an attitude of deep humility and compassion.

'What then shall we say, brothers and sisters? When you come together, each of you has a hymn, or a word of instruction, a revelation, a tongue or an interpretation. Everything must be done so that the church may be built up.' (1 Corinthians 14:26 NIV)

The Holy Spirit Course: More Than Just Words

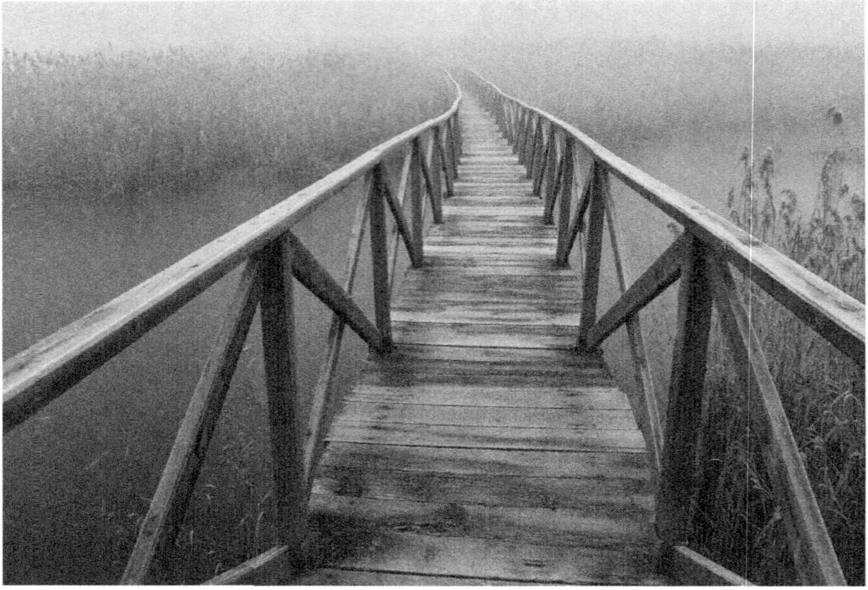

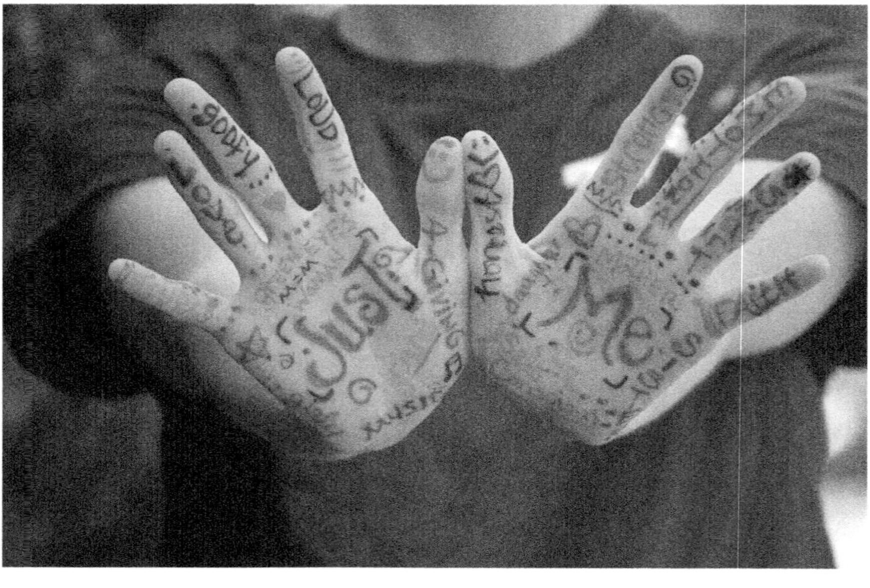
Just
Me
LOUD
GIVING

The Holy Spirit Course: More Than Just Words

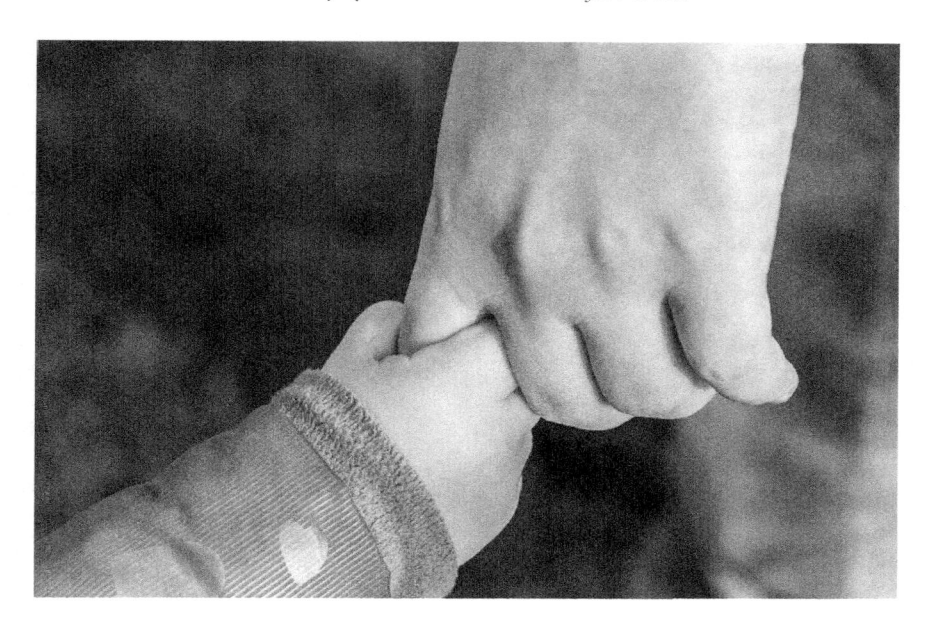

Philip Janvier

Notes:

Discussion Questions:

1. Sometimes we are challenged in ways that we are not expecting. Describe an occasion in your life when you were challenged because your expectations were not met.
2. Think of a photograph, picture, song, hymn, poem, story or piece of music that has helped you when you have been unable to express yourself fully.
3. In the Gospel of Mark Jesus stated, *"Are you not in error because you do not know the Scriptures or the power of God?" (Mark 12: 24 NIV)* What do you think he meant by this?
4. As you think back on 1 Corinthians 14 what strikes you as being startling or unexpected?
5. What do you think the Apostle Paul meant when he wrote these words? *I would like to learn just one thing from you: did you receive the Spirit by the works of the law, or by believing what you heard? (Galatians 3:2 NIV)* Think of a time when you found yourself reacting badly to an issue and then realised that you might have made a similar mistake?

Reflection on Session 8

- **What has God shown me?**

    _____
    _____

- **What do I need to ask God for?**

    _____
    _____

- **What do I need to do?**

    _____
    _____

- **Other comments.**

    _____
    _____

SESSION 9
THE HOLY SPIRIT IN WORSHIP - SUBMISSION TO GOD

Open To God 3

The Holy Spirit in Worship

- *Worship is the dramatic celebration of God in his supreme worth in such a manner that his 'worthiness' becomes the norm and inspiration of human living (Ralph P. Martin).*

- *Worship is the submission of all our nature to God. It is the quickening of the conscience by his holiness; the nourishment of the mind with his truth; the purifying of the imagination by his beauty; the opening of the heart to his love; the surrender of will to his purpose and all this gathered up in adoration, the most selfless emotion of which our nature is capable and therefore the chief remedy for that self centredness which is original sin and the source of all actual sin (William Temple)*

- Corinthians 14:26

  _____
  _____
  _____
  _____

- John 4:24

  _____
  _____
  _____
  _____

- *True worship must always be directed towards the living God. It is not a performance in order to display the talents of priests, preachers, musicians, singers, dancers or anyone else (David Watson).*

Begin with prayer and worship and invite God the Holy Spirit to come upon you and ask the Holy Spirit to give you his gifts. It is also important that everything is done in a relaxed but reverent atmosphere, providing space for people to wait on God and to take risks. Risk taking should be done in a context of love and community. Finally, it is essential that you all agree on the principle of radical honesty, that no matter how unusual, odd or strange and impression you get of God speaking that you will share it with the group and that if the message is for you, you will own it publically. For this to work there has to be an agreement of trust, that what is said in the session stays in the session and that if the revelation is deeply private, that that privacy is respected and protected.

Bible Study

Please look at the words of Jesus in **Luke 11** and Paul in **Romans 12** and ask the group or groups to answer these questions:
- What do we learn about God the Holy Spirit?
- What does it mean to be a living sacrifice?
- What do you want to ask for?
- Why did the disciples need to be taught to pray?

Please use what you have learnt in your Bible Study to help you to pray and wait on God. Remember to invite God, the Holy Spirit to come upon you and move in power.

Exercise:

Arranged on the table are a selection of randomly selected objects to be used in this Session.

- In small groups of twos or threes, each person in the group selects an object or objects, meditates and reflects over their selection.
- After this extended period, in an atmosphere of worship, love and fellowship, each person shares what they believe God, the Holy Spirit is saying to the other people in their group.
- These thoughts are then prayed over and tested in an attitude of radical honesty.
- This should be done gently and in an attitude of deep humility and compassion.

Time of Waiting

- Allow at least forty minutes for God to act and speak.
- If your group finds it helpful, play some quite worshipful music.
- Provide pens, paper and other creative items.
- There is a selection of pictures included in this book, please use a sample of them and ask your group members to look at them, and ask what God is saying to them to another person in that group.

Time of Reflection
- Thank God in advance for speaking
- Share your thoughts, images, pictures
- Ask God to reveal if they are for you
- Give the glory to God
- Close in prayer
- Allow spiritual digestion time

Notes:

Discussion Questions:

1. Christians are called to be 'Living sacrifices' discuss how this principle makes you feel and what it tells you about yourself.
2. Describe a time or occasion when you struggled to do something simple that you knew was the right thing to do.
3. Describe an occasion when you felt spiritually or emotionally blind and would have liked Jesus to teach you to pray.
4. Why do you think it is important to 'give the glory to God' when the gifts of the Spirit are evident.
5. Refer to a song, hymn, poem, story or piece of music that captures for you the essence of your submission to God.

Reflection on Session 9

- **What has God shown me?**
  _____
  _____

- **What do I need to ask God for?**
  _____
  _____

- **What do I need to do?**
  _____
  _____

- **Other comments.**
  _____
  _____

SESSION 10
THE REST OF OUR LIVES

Finally!

In Chapters 1-6 we considered God the Holy Spirit in the Old and New Testaments and have looked at the following sections:
- Who is the Holy Spirit?
- The Holy Spirit and You
- Introducing the Gifts of the Spirit
- Gifts of Revelation
    - Words of Knowledge
    - Words of Wisdom
    - Discerning of Spirits
- Gifts of Power and Authority
    - Gifts of Faith
    - Gifts of Healings
    - The working of Miracles
- Gifts of Communication
    - The Gift of Prophecy
    - The Gift of Tongues
    - The Interpretation of Tongues
- The Gifts in Practice - Open To God
    - The gifts in Worship and the Prayer of Boldness
    - The gifts in action
    - The Holy Spirit in our Worship Submission to God

A) We are the body of Christ
We are in this together, and all of us have been given gifts

Romans 12:5

1 Corinthians 12:20

B) We are connected to each other
Colossians 3:12-15

1 Corinthians 12:27

Genesis 4:8-10

_____
_____
_____

C) We are part of an incredible body
Ephesians 5:27

_____
_____
_____

D) We need to minister like Jesus
We need to be commissioned
Matthew 10:1

_____
_____
_____

Mark 16:15

_____
_____
_____

E) We are here to advance the Kingdom of God

Matthew 12:28

_____
_____

John 14:12

_____
_____
_____

F) The four types of gifting
a) **Role:** Using your natural gifts to do that which you see in the scripture.

1 Peter 4:9-11

_____
_____
_____

b) **Gift or Anointing:** The occasional use of a gift as determined by God's direction.

Acts 16:16-18

_____
_____

c) **Ministries:** As gifts are used on occasion they develop and mature into regular patterns.

Ephesians 4: 11-13 NIV

_____
_____

d) **Office:** The appointments made by God and the setting to one side by the Church for a particular purpose or function

Acts 6:2-4 NIV)

_____
_____

7) The rest of our lives
'It is a well established fact that we learn best by watching others do and then risking

doing ourselves.' (John Wimber)

The disciples had Jesus as a model to copy and then live out. The early church had the Apostles and the early disciples to copy and examples to follow. So too, we for the future growth and ministry of the church, must be living examples of what we believe.

Exercise:
On completion of this questionnaire compare your scores with those you recorded in Session 1 and consider any changes.

Test your gifts

In the first horizontal row of three squares consider the four lines that describe you best and place a number 3 in that square. Then repeat the process scoring 2 for the next appropriate and 1 for the least. Repeat this exercise for each horizontal row.

Thoughtful Intelligent Rational Open to Reason	Spontaneous Adventurous Risk-taker Explorer	Co-operative Motivator Visionary Authentic
Intuitive Confident in God Can make difficult choices I can apply spiritual truth	Explorer My prayers are answered God does the incredible in me I expect signs & wonders	Inspirational I pray in tongues God gives me messages I expect to hear God
I know when God is working I can sense the Holy Spirit I can spot fakes I can discern motives	I believe in the impossible I am confident God will act I know God's will for me I can see God in action	I want to speak for God I have understood tongues I know what God wants to say I hear God's voice
People look to me for clarity I can often see the right path I learn from scripture I read to grow in my faith	People look to me for direction God has used me I have done the impossible I act to grow in my faith	People look to me for sense God has spoken to me I expect interpretations I have asked God to use me
Others see me as wise My prayers help others I long to know more I know I am not wise	I enjoy praying for the sick Healing follows my prayer I feel special when I pray God regularly uses me	I need more words to pray My prayers come from God I am lost for words I have understanding

When all of the boxes have a number, add up the total in each vertical column and place that total in the box provided.

BOX 1	BOX 2	BOX 3

Box 1: Proclamational

- Words of Wisdom
- Words of Knowledge
- Discerning of Spirits

For God to direct his people, it is important that his people hear his voice. Therefore, it is in God's interest that we understand what he is saying. Gifts of Revelation, are the gifts God uses to communicate with his people. These gifts are not to be seen out of the context of scripture, for it is in the Bible that we find the written word of God, and any gift of revelation offered must be tested and not contradict scripture.

We are here to advance the Kingdom of God

- You want to know everything
- You love to seek out the truth, explore and share
- You find that others tell you that you have helped them from the words of scripture.
- You can be independent and nonconformist and often portray a sense of calm.
- Once you have discovered God's will, you are quite happy to let others run with the idea.
- You want to get God's word right, and justice and fairness are important to you.
- You have had insights of spiritual truth that others have found helpful.
- You study and read avidly to learn new biblical truths.
- You can distinguish when teaching is from God, from Satan, or of human origin.

Box 2: Faith In Action

- Gifts of Faith,
- Gifts of Healings
- The Working of Miracles

The gifts of Faith in Action are the foundation for all the gifts. Without it, the church would not have the confidence to act and proclaim. These gifts often go unseen. However, the gifts often achieve their outcomes because they work silently and discretely behind the scenes. These gifts are not to be seen out of the context of scripture, for it is in the Bible that we find the written word of God, and any gift of Faith in Action offered must be tested

and not contradict scripture.
We need to minister like Jesus

- You like to be free to do your own thing.
- You love to seek out the new frontiers.
- You love a challenge.
- You are not a great fan of the traditional or the safe.
- Others point to examples of your prayers resulting in observable miracles.
- God has used you personally to perform miracles and shown you signs and wonders.
- You take pleasure in praying for the sick for you know many of them will be healed.
- You can say that God has done impossible things in your life.

Box 3: Prophetic

- The Gift of Prophecy
- The Gift of Tongues
- The Interpretation of Tongues

For God to direct his people, it is important that his people hear his voice. Therefore, it is in God's interest that we hear what he is saying. Gifts of Communication are the gifts God uses to interconnect with his people. These gifts are not to be seen out of the context of scripture, for it is in the Bible that we find the written word of God, and any gift of communication offered must be tested and not contradict scripture.

We are connected to each other

- You understand the importance of relationships.
- You want to have many friends and find sharing and caring relatively easy.
- You are not afraid of your emotions and are prepared to show them.
- You have the desire to receive and pass on messages from God.
- You find praying in tongues really helpful.
- You have a strong desire to interpret tongues and offer praise to God.
- Others tell you that you have helped them hear a specific message from God.
- You have felt the presence of God and have confidence in him when significant decisions need to be made.

When everyone on your course has completed the above questionnaire enter in the results/scores for each person in the boxes below. When all of the boxes have a number, add up the total in each vertical column and place that total in the box provided.

Test your gifts

GIFTS OF REVELATION
GIFTS OF POWER AND AUTHORITY
GIFTS OF COMMUNICATION

PROCLAMATIONAL	FAITH IN ACTION	PROPHETIC

When all of the boxes have a number, add up the total in each vertical column and place that total in the box provided.

PROCLAMATIONAL	FAITH IN ACTION	PROPHETIC

The totals above will then suggest the strengths and weaknesses in your fellowship and give an indication of your teaching needs. It is often the case that a church or fellowship, may be strong in one or two areas but weak in a third. For example, the fellowship may be strong in the proclamation of the gospel but weak in putting it into action. Strong in the prophetic but weak in sharing. Strong in social action but weak in the prophetic and proclamational.

Conclusion

We are the body of Christ. We are in this together, and all of us have been given gifts, even if our score is low, we still have our gifts.

The four types of gifting
1. Role: Using your natural gifts to do that which you see in the scripture.
2. Gift or Anointing: The occasional use of a gift as determined by God's direction.
3. Ministries: As gifts are used on occasion they develop and mature into regular patterns.
4. Office: The appointments made by God and the setting to one side by the Church for a particular purpose or function

What Next?
Having discovered in what area our gifts are in is only the beginning of our spiritual journey and our relationship with God. The challenge for us is to attempt to live out these attributes of God in our daily lives. That means being aware of our weaknesses, as well as our strengths.

It may well be that we have proclamational gifts and that we have an understanding of the spiritual gifts of knowledge, wisdom and discernment. But that may mean that we are weak in gifts of power and authority or communication. Prayerfully, we need to discover how to develop our gifts and grow in our love and experience of God. However, all of the gifts of God the Holy Spirit are intended to build up the whole church, and as such, our areas of weakness will be somebody else's area of strength.

Two questions seem to leap out at me from these pages:
What energises each group? & What drains each group?

At the end of this Holy Spirit Course, and having completed this questionnaire, we may well discover that the majority of our fellowship have skills and gifts in one or two out of the three areas. Our church may be strong in proclamation but weak in the prophetic and visionary. We may be strong in the prophetic but weak in putting our faith into action and so on.

"But he said to me, 'My grace is sufficient for you, for my power is made perfect in weakness.' Therefore I will boast all the more gladly about my weaknesses, so that Christ's power may rest on me."
(2 Corinthians 12:9 NIV)

Discussion Questions:

1. Describe how you feel when you read these words, *Now you are the body of Christ, and each one of you is a part of it. (1 Corinthians 12:27 NIV)*
2. Read these words of Jesus and consider what the implications for us today are? *Very truly I tell you, whoever believes in me will do the works I have been doing, and they will do even greater things than these, because I am going to the Father. (John 14:12 NIV)*
3. The disciples' hearts burned with enthusiasm after the Day of Pentecost. Describe a time when you suddenly were filled with unexpected hope or joy.
4. Describe a time when you felt God was speaking to someone through you. Consider your words and how they might apply to yourself.
5. If it is true that God, can use you and give you his gifts, how does that impact on your plans for tomorrow, this week and the months ahead?

Notes:

Reflection on Session 10

- What has God shown me?

- What do I need to ask God for?

- What do I need to do?

- Other comments.

APPENDIX

Section 1

Good practice in the ministry of healing.

In 2000 the House of Bishops of the Church of England agreed to the publication on its behalf of the House of Bishops' guidelines for good practice in the healing ministry. While these guidelines were issued to the Church of England, I believe that they do generally apply to the church of God. The following is a summary of those findings:

The healing ministry is Jesus' ministry entrusted to us, always to be exercised with reverence, love and compassion. The guiding principle is to recognise the presence of God in those receiving this ministry and honour his presence in them.

1. **Prayer and preparation.** The healing ministry is based on prayer in the name of Jesus Christ; those involved in this ministry should be prayerful, regularly practicing Christians who acknowledge his healing love and are willing to pray and listen for guidance in order to minister appropriately to others.
2. **Safety.** All reasonable steps should be taken to ensure the safety of the person receiving this ministry. People have a right to know what is being provided and how they will be ministered to.
3. **Accountability and diocesan regulations.** Everyone involved in the healing ministry needs clear lines of accountability to recognize who holds relevant authority within their parish church. All reasonable steps should be taken by those involved to ensure their awareness of current law as it applies to this ministry, e.g. data protection, informed consent. Legal liability issues must be considered from an insurance viewpoint. Existing diocesan regulations should be also followed.
4. **Training.** Individuals should receive appropriate training in this ministry and be kept up to date with developments and its ecumenical expression. Healing team leaders must ensure that members have opportunities for training and a common understanding of good practice.
5. **Competence and boundaries.** Persons in this ministry should be aware of their personal limitations and ensure that

6. **Personal conduct**. The healing ministry is part of the message of the gospel; the personal conduct of everyone involved should encourage confidence in this ministry and not undermine it. Language, personal hygiene, general appearance, body language and touch used by those ministering should be appropriate, considerate and courteous towards those receiving it. No-one should be ministered to against their will.
7. **Confidentiality and public statements.** People's privacy and dignity should be respected and protected. Any limitations to confidentiality should be explained in advance and any disclosure should be restricted to relevant information. It should be conveyed only to appropriate people, normally with the parishioner's consent, and not misused in any way.
8. **Counselling and psychotherapy.** These specific treatments, as distinct from pastoral care and listening, should only be provided by accredited counsellors and therapists who adhere to the codes of ethics and practice of their regulatory organizations and who have professional insurance cover.
9. **Deliverance.** The House of Bishops' guidelines (1975) should be followed and diocesan advisors consulted when necessary.
10. **Partnership.** The healing ministry should be carried out in co-operation, where appropriate, with chaplains and representatives of our ecumenical partners, and those involved in professional and voluntary healthcare, whilst recognizing that they may be bound by other codes of conduct.

Copyright © The Archbishops' Council 2000, from the report A Time to Heal.

APPENDIX

Section 2

Are there Spiritual Gifts today or have they Ceased?

It is clear from the title and contents of this book that I believe that the Gifts of the Holy Spirit are for today. However, there is an opposing view, that the Spiritual Gifts were limited to the period of the New Testament and ended there.

Dr Peter Masters, in his article, Cessationsim - Proving Charismatic Gifts have Ceased (2011) states: *We believe, however, that the ceasing of revelatory and sign-gifts in the time of the apostles is very plainly taught in God's Word, so plainly, in fact, that the opposite view has only seriously appeared in the last 100 years or so.'*

It is true that in the last 100 years or so, there has been a rediscovery of God the Holy Spirit and the gifts that he gives. However, to imply that such spiritual gifts have been absent from the Christian Church, is a fallacy. E. H. Broadbent, in his fascinating - if hard going - book, The Pilgrim Church, documents many examples of the movements of the Holy Spirit in the Church.

However, there are many who disagree on both sides, how can we coexist?

For those who believe the gifts are no longer for today, Dr Peter Masters continues, *We sincerely pray that God will deliver those who are his true children from the accumulating harm of this wildly mistaken departure from Scripture. It is perfectly possible to prove that cessationism is a Biblical truth.*

For those of us, who disagree with such a view, my conclusion, is to quote the words of Jesus in Matthew 7:16, *By their fruit you will recognise them. Do people pick grapes from thorn-bushes, or figs from thistles? (NIV).*

By your fruit you will be known.

We are defined by our words and actions. Therefore, the way we coexist with those who disagree with us is important. I urge all who claim to be disciples of the Lord Jesus Christ, to live in love and peace with each other. In the words of a fellow minister of mine, who holds a disagreeing view, *'Make the main things, the main thing. You must be born again and you must be filled with the Spirit.'* If we can live out these words of scripture, then we will be indeed, making the main the things the main thing!

"Love the Lord your God with all your heart and with all your soul and with all your mind.' [38] *This is the first and greatest commandment.* [39] *And the second is like it: "Love*

your neighbour as yourself.' ⁴⁰ All the Law and the Prophets hang on these two commandments.' (Matthew 22:37-38 NIV).

Where does that leave us?
I do understand that there are occasions, when Biblically minded, pure-hearted, sincere and honest, Godly-people, disagree. When that happens, all we can do is pray and ask our Almighty, God and Father, to forgive us and to fall back onto the words and wisdom of Jesus:

'My prayer is not for them alone. I pray also for those who will believe in me through their message, that all of them may be one, Father, just as you are in me and I am in you. May they also be in us so that the world may believe that you have sent me. I have given them the glory that you gave me, that they may be one as we are one – I in them and you in me – so that they may be brought to complete unity. Then the world will know that you sent me and have loved them even as you have loved me.' (John 17:20-23 NIV)

May God bless you this day.
Philip Janvier

APPENDIX

Section 3

FEEDBACK FORM

It is always good practice at the end of a course such as this that those participating in it have a chance to feedback their experiences. I suggest something like the example below is used.

THE HOLY SPIRIT COURSE: MORE THAN JUST WORDS

Feedback Form

Thank you for taking part in **THE HOLY SPIRIT COURSE: MORE THAN JUST WORDS** ten-week training course. I hope that you have enjoyed the sessions and would like to ask you to give a little feedback. Your honest feedback will help us to make the course even better and enable us to correct some of its shortfalls. Thank you.

Name: _____ [Only if you are prepared to be quoted]

	Excellent	Good	Fair	Poor
1. Who is the Holy Spirit?	☐	☐	☐	☐
2. The Holy Spirit and You	☐	☐	☐	☐
3. Introducing the Gifts of the Holy Spirit	☐	☐	☐	☐
4. Gifts of Revelation	☐	☐	☐	☐
5. Gifts of Power and Authority	☐	☐	☐	☐
6. Gifts of Communication	☐	☐	☐	☐
7. Open to God 1: The Gifts in Worship and the prayer of Boldness	☐	☐	☐	☐
8. Open to God 2: The Gifts in Action	☐	☐	☐	☐
9. Open to God: 3 Submission to God	☐	☐	☐	☐
10. The rest of our lives	☐	☐	☐	☐
11. The PowerPoint Presentation	☐	☐	☐	☐
12. The Member's Manual	☐	☐	☐	☐
13. The Handouts	☐	☐	☐	☐
14. The Holy Spirit Course: More than just words (COMPLETE COURSE)	☐	☐	☐	☐

Your comments:
_____
_____
_____
_____
_____

Signature _____ (Only if you are prepared to be quoted)   Date: _____

REFERENCES

- Archbishops' Council, A Time to Heal: The Development of Good Practice in the Healing Ministry: A Handbook, 2013, SCM
- Barth Karl, quoted in J.J. von Allmen, Worship: Its Theology and Practice, London: 1965 Lutterworth,
- Bennett, Denis and Rita, The Holy Spirit And You, 1979, Kingsway
- Broadbent, Edmund Hamer, The Pilgrim Church, 1931, Marshall

Pickering
- Calver, Clive, The Holy Spirit, 1984, Scripture Union
- Green, Michael, I Believe in the Holy Spirit, 1975, Hodder & Stoughton
- Gunstone, John, The Lord is Our Healer, 1986, Hodder & Stoughton
- Healing Ministry, The… A Time and Place to Heal, The Anglican Healing Ministry Website, 2017, http://www.healingministry.org.uk
- Maddox Bishop: Twenty Questions about Healing, London 1981, SPCK
- Masters, Peter, Cessationism - Proving Charismatic Gifts have Ceased, The Sword & Trowel, 2011 Issue 2, http://www.metropolitantabernacle.org/Christian-Article/Cessationism-Proving-Charismatic-Gifts-have-Ceased-Sword-and-Trowel-Magazine
- Packer, J.I., Keep in Step with the Spirit, 1984, 2005, Grand Rapids: Revell
- Peck, John, What The Bible Says About The Holy Spirit, 1979, Kingsway
- Piper John, The New Testament Gift of Prophecy, Definition, Theses and Suggestions, 1990, http://www.desiringgod.org/articles/the-new-testament-gift-of-prophecy
- Pytches, David, Come Holy Spirit, 1985, Hodder & Stoughton
- Roxburgh, Robert L, Renewal Down To Earth, 1987, Kingsway
- Smail, Tom, Reflected Glory, 1975, Hodder & Stoughton
- Smail, Tom, The Giving Gift, 1988, Hodder & Stoughton
- Wagner, Peter C, Your Spiritual Gifts Can Help Your Church Grow, 1979-2012. Regal Books
- Walker, Tom, Renew Us By Your Holy Spirit, 1982, Hodder & Stoughton
- Watson, David, One In The Spirit, 1973, Hodder & Stoughton
- Wimber and Springer, John and Kevin, Power Healing, 1987, HarperCollins

FINAL WORDS

E. Stanley Jones, the great missionary pioneer, used to say that evangelism was one beggar telling another where to find bread. It is as we allow the Holy Spirit to control our lives that he reminds us of the message and provides the resources and encouragement for its delivery. No one would pretend that encouragement for its delivery. No one would pretend that such lives are easy, but they are fruitful. Perhaps, by the Spirit's help, we might even end up echoing C.T. Studd's famous words.

"O let us not rust out let us not glide through the world and then slip quietly out, without having even blown the trumpets loud and long for our blessed Redeemer. At the very least let us see to it that the Devil holds a thanksgiving service in hell when he gets the news of our departure from the field of battle.'" *(Clive Calver The Holy Spirit)*

ABOUT THE AUTHOR

Philip Janvier is the Team Rector of St Stephen's Gateacre, Liverpool in the United Kingdom. He helped to found Liverpool Youth For Christ and has spoken at

Spring Harvest.

Currently, he is the Chair of Trustees of, Liverpool City Centre Street Pastors. He was born in Liverpool in 1957 and studied Theology at Trinity College, Bristol.

He is the author of the best-selling, 'Encounters with Jesus: Writing in the sand.' He is an award-winning documentary videographer, and he is the author of the Children's Fantasy series, 'The Fin Butler Adventures.'

Before becoming a minister, author and videographer, Phil worked in a photographic laboratory, as a photographer and spent nine years working in a ship's agent.

He is married and lives in Liverpool where he is addicted to music, reading, loves children's fantasy novels and Doctor Who.

ALSO BY THE AUTHOR

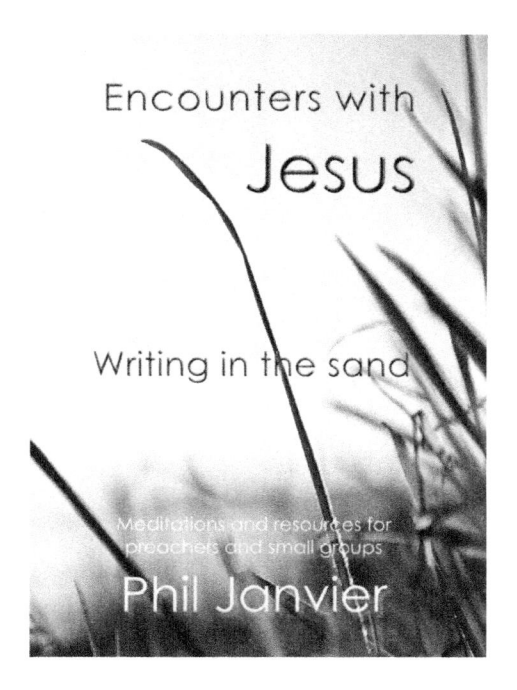

This book is aimed at:
- Those who want to go slightly deeper into gospel stories but are not sure how.
- Those who want to meditate and imagine that they were really there. To smell the salt in the air and hear the banter of the disciples.
- Providing resources for preachers, leaders and small groups.

Each chapter is broken down into three sections; the story, study and questions. I had in mind something that would bring the bible alive, empower discussion and provide thought provoking questions that were open ended, accessible to all and at times be slightly uncomfortable.

AVAILABLE FREE AS AN EBOOK ON ALL MAJOR PLATFORMS
https://www.books2read.com/u/3LrxLM
https://www.amazon.co.uk/Encounters-Jesus-Writing-Phil-Janvier/dp/1492781444
https://www.amazon.com/Encounters-Jesus-Writing-Phil-Janvier/dp/1492781444

Also available on Amazon as a paperback (ISBN-10: 1492781444, ISBN-13: 978-1492781448)

Printed in Great Britain
by Amazon